Palgrave Studies in Classical Liberalism

This series offers a forum to writers concerned that the central presuppositions of the liberal tradition have been severely corroded, neglected, or misappropriated by overly rationalistic and constructivist approaches.

The hardest-won achievement of the liberal tradition has been the wrestling of epistemic independence from overwhelming concentrations of power, monopolies and capricious zealotries. The very precondition of knowledge is the exploitation of the epistemic virtues accorded by society's situated and distributed manifold of spontaneous orders, the DNA of the modern civil condition.

With the confluence of interest in situated and distributed liberalism emanating from the Scottish tradition, Austrian and behavioral economics, non-Cartesian philosophy and moral psychology, the editors are soliciting proposals that speak to this multidisciplinary constituency. Sole or joint authorship submissions are welcome as are edited collections, broadly theoretical or topical in nature.

Peter de Marneffe

The Myth of Classical Liberalism

How Political Identity Evolves

palgrave
macmillan

Peter de Marneffe
Arizona State University
Tempe, AZ, USA

ISSN 2662-6470 ISSN 2662-6489 (electronic)
Palgrave Studies in Classical Liberalism
ISBN 978-3-032-14318-1 ISBN 978-3-032-14319-8 (eBook)
https://doi.org/10.1007/978-3-032-14319-8

This Palgrave Macmillan imprint is published by the registered company Springer Nature Switzerland AG.
The registered company address is: Gewerbestrasse 11, 6330 Cham, Switzerland

For Sally

Acknowledgments I thank the following people for comments on earlier drafts: Sally Ball, Sean Beienberg, Calvin Schermerhorn, Trevor Shelley, Henry Thomson, Jonathan Quong, Paul Weithman, Leif Wenar, and an anonymous reviewer for Palgrave Macmillan. I thank the librarians at the Arizona State University Library for access to many of the texts cited in this work.

Competing Interests The author has no competing interests to declare that are relevant to the content of this manuscript.

Contents

About the Author

Peter de Marneffe teaches philosophy at Arizona State University. He is the author of *Liberalism and Prostitution* and, with Douglas Husak, *The Legalization of Drugs*.

1

Introduction

Abstract This chapter introduces "the myth of classical liberalism," which consists of two main claims. First, the English word "liberalism" originally referred to the free market philosophy of Adam Smith. Second, Franklin Roosevelt changed the meaning of the word "liberalism" during the New Deal by using the term "liberals" to refer to supporters of his New Deal policies. Both claims are false. This is shown in the following chapters with a "word history" of the English words "liberals" and "liberalism" in nineteenth-century England and early twentieth-century America.

Keywords History of liberalism · Classical liberalism · Libertarianism · F. A. Hayek · Franklin D. Roosevelt · New Deal

In *The Conscience of a Conservative*, published in 1960, Senator Barry Goldwater embraced a political ideology that only a quarter century earlier had been labeled "liberalism" by his recent political ancestors,

P. de Marneffe, *The Myth of Classical Liberalism*, Palgrave Studies in Classical Liberalism,
https://doi.org/10.1007/978-3-032-14319-8_1

Herbert Hoover and Robert Taft.[1] So why didn't he entitle this book "The Conscience of a Liberal"?

In 1978, F.A. Hayek and Ronald Dworkin, two influential political philosophers, each published an essay entitled "Liberalism," purporting to tell us what liberalism is. According to Hayek, liberalism is the view that coercive government power should be exercised only to enforce rules of interpersonal justice,[2] a view sometimes called "libertarianism." According to Dworkin, liberalism is "a theory of equality that requires official neutrality amongst theories of what is valuable in life."[3] These are very different views. According to Hayek, liberalism is incompatible with government policies adopted to reduce income inequality. According to Dworkin, liberalism *requires* policies of this kind.[4] How did the same word with the same history in the same language come to mean such different things in the same year to two erudite men with a strong command of the English language?

In 1884, Herbert Spencer, one of the most influential political philosophers of the late nineteenth century, maintained that only libertarianism is "true liberalism."[5] A century later, in 1996, John Rawls, the most influential political philosopher of the late twentieth century,

[1] Barry Goldwater, *The Conscience of a Conservative* (Shepherdsville, KY: Victor Publishing, 1960); Herbert Hoover, "Campaign Address, New York City," October 22, 1928, *Hoover Archives*, https://hoover.archives.gov/sites/default/files/research/ebooks/b2v1_full.pdf, 583; Herbert Hoover, "Address at Madison Square Garden in New York City," October 31, 1932, *Public Papers of the Presidents of the United States: Herbert Hoover*, 1932–1933 (Office of the Federal Register National Archives and Records Service General Administration, 1977), 676; Robert A. Taft, "Liberalism—Real or New Deal?" *Young Republican* 1 (May 1936); Robert A. Taft, "What is a Liberal?" *Commercial and Financial Chronicle* 163, no. 4491 (1946).

[2] F.A. Hayek, "Liberalism," in *New Studies in Philosophy, Politics, Economics and the History of Ideas* (Chicago: University of Chicago Press, 1978), 132, 135, 144. See, too, F.A. Hayek, "The Principles of a Liberal Social Order," in *Studies in Philosophy, Politics, and Economics* (Chicago: University of Chicago Press, 1967).

[3] Ronald Dworkin, "Liberalism," in *Public and Private Morality*, ed. Stuart Hampshire (New York: Cambridge University Press, 1978), 142.

[4] Dworkin, "Liberalism," 128–33.

[5] Herbert Spencer, "The New Toryism," in *The Man Versus the State* (Indianapolis, IN: Liberty Fund, 1982), 26. Originally published in 1884.

maintained that libertarianism is "not liberalism at all."[6] How did this happen?

A common answer is this: Nineteenth-century liberals were united by two commitments, limited constitutional government and laissez-faire economic principles. "Liberalism" was originally the name for this ideological synthesis.[7] But during the New Deal, President Franklin D. Roosevelt used the words "liberals" and "liberalism" in a new way. As a result, the term "liberalism" came to be understood as the doctrine that the government should actively manage the economy and oversee the distribution of wealth; "liberals" were those who supported Roosevelt's New Deal policies, and "conservatives" were those who opposed them. Spencer, Hoover, Taft, and Hayek, all used the term "liberalism" properly to refer to the original anti-interventionist economic doctrine of the nineteenth century, which has come to be known as "classical liberalism." But after Roosevelt effectively changed the meaning of the word, "liberalism" was understood to refer to a social democratic political ideology, fundamentally opposed in its essentials to the original, classical doctrine, and this is how Dworkin and Rawls used the term. Goldwater, who embraced the anti-interventionist view, but who understood that the term "liberalism" had been coopted in this way, rejected the "liberal" label and called himself a "conservative" instead, to make clear that he favored limited government.

I call this story "the myth of classical liberalism" because it is inaccurate in two key respects. First, "liberalism" was not originally the name for the laissez-faire economic doctrine. Second, Roosevelt did not change the meaning of the words in the 1930s. To support these claims, I recount here the early history of the English words "liberals" and "liberalism" in nineteenth-century England and early twentieth-century America. This, in short, is the story I tell:

The plural noun "liberals" entered English in the early nineteenth century as a label for those who supported or sympathized with

---

[6] John Rawls, *Political Liberalism*, paperback ed. (New York: Columbia University Press, 1996), lviii.

[7] A short version of this mythical story is presented in Milton Friedman, *Capitalism and Freedom* (Chicago: University of Chicago Press, 1962), 7.

constitutionalist or republican political movements on the European continent, movements which aimed either to limit monarchical power with a written constitution or to replace monarchy with representative government. In the 1820s, the term "liberals" came to refer to a pro-reform clique within the Tory ministry of Lord Liverpool, and then, after the Reform Act of 1832, it came to refer more generally to those who identified themselves as reformers—those who supported electoral and other legal and economic reforms. Not long after, the term "liberals" came to refer to members of the unofficially named "liberal party," a parliamentary coalition of Whigs, Radicals, Repealers, and Reformers—terms explained below in Chap. 2—which was formed in opposition to the newly named Conservative Party of Sir Robert Peel. Because this liberal party came to be characterized in the 1840s by an almost unanimous consensus on the abolition of the Corn Laws—protective tariffs on imported grains—the term "liberals" was subsequently understood to refer to those in favor of abolishing these tariffs; and then, because many of these persons also supported free trade as a matter of general principle, it came to refer to those in favor of free trade; and then, because some of these also opposed all government intervention into the economy, the term came to refer to those opposed to all such intervention. This course of events has produced the misperception that all self-identified liberals in the nineteenth century opposed government intervention into the economy, but already in the early 1840s some members of "the liberal party" favored laws limiting factory hours[8] and by the 1880s a sharp disagreement had developed among self-identified liberals about what liberalism "really" was, some identifying it with principled opposition to government intervention, others arguing that it *required* some forms of intervention. This disagreement about the nature of liberalism persisted into the twentieth century and was echoed a half-century later in the United States.

[8] Joseph Coohill, *Ideas of the Liberal Party: Perceptions, Agendas and Liberal Politics in the House of Commons, 1832–1852* (Oxford: Wiley-Blackwell, 2011), 60; Norman Gash, *Sir Robert Peel: The Life of Sir Robert Peel after 1830* (London: Longman, 1972), 438–39; Peter Mandler, *Aristocratic Government in the Age of Reform, Whigs and Liberals, 1830–1852* (New York: Oxford University Press, 1990), 222, 240; Robert B. McCallum, *The Liberal Party from Earl Grey to Asquith* (London: Victor Gollancz, 1961), 41.

The noun "liberals" was not an important part of American political discourse in the nineteenth century, which is understandable given the political origin of the English word. Early nineteenth-century European liberals were those opposed to absolute monarchy and in favor of either constitutional monarchy or republican government. Because the War of Independence established a constitutional republican government in America, there was no need for a liberal party in the U.S. However, the same ideological split between government interventionists and anti-interventionists that emerged in Britain in the late nineteenth century emerged in the U.S. too, under different labels, with the words "progressives" and "radicals" referring to the interventionists, and the words "conservatives," "standpatters," and "reactionaries," referring to the anti-interventionists. Then in the first few decades of the twentieth-century, Americans increasingly used the terms "progressive" and "liberal" interchangeably, so that by the time Roosevelt began to refer to supporters of his interventionist New Deal policies as "liberals" and to its opponents as "conservatives," he was relying on an established American usage. It is an error, then, to say, as some have suggested,[9] that Roosevelt changed the meaning of the term, and it is this usage by Roosevelt that provides the foundation for how we use the terms "liberals" and "conservatives" in the U.S. today.[10] In what follows, I tell this story in greater detail, with textual support.

What follows is an example of what Helena Rosenblatt has called a "word history of liberalism"[11] and she maintains that it is only by studying the history of the words "liberals" and "liberalism" that we can understand the history of liberalism. I agree, but unlike Rosenblatt I

---

[9] Christopher Ellis and James A. Stimson, "Symbolic Ideology in the American Electorate," *Electoral Studies* 28, no. 3 (2009), 397; Verlan Lewis, *Ideas of Power* (New York: Cambridge University Press, 2019), 123; Seymour Martin Lipset, "Americans Sneer at Liberalism. Why?" *New York Times*, October 28, 1988; Sidney M. Milkis *The President and the Parties* (New York: Oxford University Press, 1993), 49; Justin Vaïsse, *Neoconservativism: The Biography of a Movement*, trans. Arthur Goldhammer (Cambridge, MA: Harvard University Press, 2010), 6.

[10] See Hyrum Lewis and Verlan Lewis, *The Myth of Left and Right* (New York: Oxford University Press, 2023) for an account of the evolution in the American meaning of "liberals" and "liberalism" since the New Deal.

[11] Helena Rosenblatt, *The Lost History of Liberalism: From Ancient Rome to the Twenty-First Century* (Princeton, NJ: Princeton University Press, 2018), 3.

do not focus here on the history of these words in French. This is because my primary aim is to understand how the English words "liberals" and "liberalism" acquired such different and conflicting meanings in twentieth-century America and I believe this can be understood without attending to French usage. This, too, is why I say nothing about the history of these words in other English-speaking nations, such as Canada, Australia, and New Zealand.

What led me to this research was puzzlement about the inconsistent and confusing ways in which "liberal" came to be used in twentieth-century American English. When I looked for a satisfying explanation, I was unable to find one. So I started digging, and what follows is what I found. My primary aim is to understand what happened: how did the same English word with the same history come to mean such different things? But another aim is to debunk a rhetorical strategy employed by classical liberals and libertarians in support of their favored views, which is to identify libertarianism as "true liberalism," "real liberalism," or "liberalism in its original sense."[12] The term "classical liberalism" suggests there is something pure and unadulterated about this form of liberalism and that what came to be called "liberalism" in twentieth-century America is a corruption. If the term "liberalism" is now used to refer to social democratic principles and policies only as a result of rhetorical trickery by a wily demagogue who knew how to manipulate a naïve American public, this (somehow) seems a point in favor of the classical doctrine. But if, as I contend, this story is a myth, and Roosevelt engaged in no trickery in applying the term "liberalism" to his New Deal

[12] Hoover identifies classical liberalism as "true liberalism" in Herbert Hoover, "True Liberalism," in *Addresses Upon the American Road* (New York: Charles Scribner's Sons, 1938), 126. Hayek identifies classical liberalism as "true liberalism" in F.A. Hayek, *The Constitution of Liberty* (Chicago: University of Chicago Press, 1960), 407. Friedman identifies classical liberalism as the creed of "true liberals" and "liberalism in its original sense" in Friedman, *Capitalism and Freedom*, 8–9. For a recent example of this rhetorical strategy, see Deirdre McCloskey, *Why Liberalism Works* (New Haven, CT: Yale University Press, 2019), ix–7, equating "true liberalism" with libertarianism. Though not a libertarian, Samuel Moyn briefly embraces a version of the myth of classical liberalism where he writes, "Before the Cold War, liberalism largely served as an apologia for *laissez-faire* economic policies." See Samuel Moyn, *Liberalism Against Itself* (New Haven, CT: Yale University Press, 2023), 2–3.

policies, then what we now call "classical liberalism" is no more the genuine article than New Deal liberalism is.

In 1848, C.G. Lewis wrote in the *Edinburgh Review*: "When we speak of *a liberal system of government*—a phrase, we confess, which is not very precise we mean such a system of government as is indicated by the opinions of the old Whig Party of England, improved and enlarged by modern speculation, particularly in questions of public economy and jurisprudence."[13] This is how Hayek understood what he called "classical British liberalism" a century later,[14] characterizing it as "the doctrine of the Old Whigs and of Adam Smith."[15] In challenging the myth of classical liberalism, I do not deny that "liberalism" was understood in nineteenth-century England to encompass the constitutionalist views of the Old Whigs and Smith's principles of political economy, but I do argue that this was not how most self-identified British liberals understood their own views or how most self-identified British liberals understood the term "liberalism." For this reason, Hayek's term "classical British liberalism" is misleading if it leads one to conclude that what is now called "classical liberalism" is what all nineteenth-century Britons originally understood the term "liberalism" to mean.

The normative validity of a political doctrine does not depend on what it was first called. So even if the myth of classical liberalism is false, it does not follow that social democratic versions of liberalism are morally superior to classical versions, and if this myth were true, it would not follow that classical liberalism is morally superior to social democratic views. But whatever our ideological orientation, we might be curious about how it is that an English word that had one clear meaning a century and a half ago came to mean its virtual opposite a 100 years later. The answer is that it didn't. The English word "liberalism" never unambiguously referred either to classical liberalism or libertarianism, as shown in the following chapters.[16]

---

[13] C.G. Lewis, Review of "Letter from Sir Robert Peel to the Electors for the Borough of Tamworth," *Edinburgh Review* 87 (1848), 152.

[14] Hayek, "Liberalism," 128.

[15] Hayek, "Liberalism," 125.

[16] "Libertarianism" and "classical liberalism" are commonly understood to refer to different, though related, views, but what I am calling "the myth of classical liberalism" has been taken to

This is an essay in political history, specifically the history of political rhetoric; it is not an intellectual history of liberalism or a history of ideas. The history of an idea identifies when this idea first arose, under what social conditions, how the understanding of this idea changed over time, and how it has been realized institutionally. A history of the idea of democracy, for example, would identify when this idea first arose, in what social context, how it was understood then, how it was institutionally realized then if it was, and how it has been understood and institutionally realized since then. Many different ideas have been identified with liberalism: the idea of republican government; the idea of democracy; the idea of constitutional government; the idea of representative government; the idea of freedom of inquiry; the idea of freedom of conscience; the idea of freedom of expression; the idea of free markets; the idea of private property rights; the idea that social institutions should be designed to achieve the greatest happiness for the greatest number; the idea that each person has an inherent value on the basis of which he or she has rights and is entitled to equal respect; the Kantian principle of equal liberty that a person's liberty may be restricted by law only to protect an equal liberty for others; the Millian principle of liberty that a person's liberty may be restricted only to protect others from harm; the idea that social and political institutions should be arranged so as to promote human progress and development; the idea of equal opportunity; the idea that the government has an obligation to provide basic material security; the idea that the government should act to reduce inequalities in wealth; the idea that the government should be neutral between competing ideals of the good life; and more. Because so many different ideas have been identified with liberalism, a complete history of liberalism would include a history of each of these ideas, some of which are more than 2000 years old. This is certainly worth doing, but it is not

---

support libertarian views as well as classical liberal views. In Chap. 6, I explain what I take the difference between classical liberalism and libertarianism to be. For helpful discussion of the differences between them (and of different forms of libertarianism), see Matt Zwolinski and John Tomasi, *The Individualists* (Princeton, NJ: Princeton University Press, 2023), Chap. 1; Samuel Freeman, "Illiberal Libertarians: Why Libertarianism Is Not a Liberal View," *Philosophy & Public Affairs* 30, no. 2 (2001): 105–51; Samuel Freeman, "Capitalism in the Classical and High Liberal Traditions," *Social Philosophy and Policy* 28, no. 2 (2011): 19–55.

what I am doing here. I aim to address two questions that are much more specific. How did the English words "liberals" and "liberalism" come to have such different meanings over the past two centuries? And did the English word "liberalism" originally refer to the free market principles of Adam Smith, as suggested by the myth of classical liberalism? To answer these questions, it is not necessary to know the history of the pre-nineteenth-century ideas that are now commonly identified with liberalism; nor would knowing this history help.

Intellectual histories of liberalism also raise questions they do not always answer. A standard history identifies liberalism with several key ideas and tells a history of these ideas,[17] but it rarely explains why the author identifies *these* particular ideas with "liberalism" or why the author takes these ideas to be the most important ones, which leads the reader to wonder, what is it in the history of this word or in the author's personal biography that led the author to identify these particular ideas with liberalism or to regard them as central? Does the author take these ideas as central to liberalism because the author sees himself or herself as "a liberal" and these ideas are central to the author's own conception of political morality? Or does the author take these ideas as central to liberalism because the author sees himself or herself as an anti-

[17] Some examples are Anthony Arblaster, *The Rise and Decline of Western Liberalism* (Oxford: Basil Blackwell, 1984); W. Lyon Blease, *A Short History of English Liberalism* (London: T. Fisher Unwin, 1913); Nancy Cohen, *The Reconstruction of American Liberalism, 1865–1914* (Chapel Hill, NC: University of North Carolina Press, 2002); Robert Eccleshall, *British Liberalism: Liberal Thought from the 1640s to 1980s* (New York: Longman, 1986); Edmund Fawcett, *Liberalism: The Life of an Idea*, 2nd ed. (Princeton, NJ: Princeton University Press, 2018); Michael Freeden, *Liberalism: A Very Short Introduction* (New York: Oxford University Press, 2015); Gerald Gaus, *The Modern Liberal Theory of Man* (London: Routledge, 1983); John Gray, *Liberalism*, 2nd ed. (Minneapolis, MN: University of Minnesota Press, 1995); John H. Hallowell, *The Decline of Liberalism as an Ideology, with Particular Reference to German Politico-Legal Thought* (Berkeley, CA: University of California Press, 1943); Louis Hartz, *The Liberal Tradition in America* (New York: Harcourt, Brace, 1955); Harold J. Laski, *The Rise of European Liberalism* (London: Unwin, 1962); Domenico Losurdo, *Liberalism: A Counter-History*, trans. Gregory Elliot (London: Verso, 2011); Thomas P. Neill, *The Rise and Decline of Liberalism* (Milwaukee, WI: Bruce Publishing, 1953); Rosenblatt, *The Lost History of Liberalism*; Guido de Ruggiero, *The History of European Liberalism*, trans. R.G. Collingwood (Oxford: Oxford University Press, 1927); Alan Ryan, *The Making of Modern Liberalism* (Princeton, NJ: Princeton University Press, 2012); George H. Smith, *The System of Liberty: Themes in the History of Classical Liberalism* (New York: Cambridge University Press, 2013); and Harold Stearns, *Liberalism in America: Its Origins, Its Temporary Collapse, Its Future* (New York: Boni and Liveright, 1919).

liberal and sees these ideas as especially pernicious? Or did the author simply learn to use the word "liberalism" in graduate school to refer to a certain kind of view and never wondered why? If we approach the history of liberalism by looking at the history of the English words "liberals" and "liberalism," this will certainly not tell us everything we want to know about the history of the ideas identified with liberalism, but it will help each of us to understand how it came about that we use these ambiguous terms in the way we do.

In the next chapter, I present the early history of the English noun "liberal," as used to ascribe a political identity to oneself, and argue that it originally identified a person as a constitutionalist or a republican. In the chapter after that, I examine the early history of the English word "liberalism" and show that it was not generally understood in nineteenth-century England to refer to the economic principles of Adam Smith and David Ricardo or to a libertarian theory of government. In Chap. 4, I examine Hayek's identification of nineteenth-century British liberalism with the views of Smith and Ricardo and explain in greater detail why this understanding of nineteenth-century liberalism is undermined by the evidence. Hayek's history has recently been defended by Daniel Klein, an economic historian, but the facts presented by Klein are too far removed from the nineteenth century to illuminate how the terms "liberals" and "liberalism" were understood then.[18] In Chap. 5, I debunk another element of the myth of classical liberalism, which is that Roosevelt changed the meanings of the terms "liberals" and "liberalism" so that they came to mean "the opposite" of what they had originally meant. In Chap. 6, I say something about the history of the term "classical liberalism" and maintain that although it is useful in picking out one version of liberalism, we should not allow it to mislead us into thinking that this version of liberalism is what all nineteenth-century liberals endorsed. Then, in conclusion, I say something about the way the words "liberals" and "liberalism" have been used in America since the New Deal.

[18] Daniel Klein, "'Liberal' as a Political Adjective (in English), 1769–1824," *Journal of Contextual Economics—Schmollers Jahrbuch* 143 (2024): 239–61, https://doi.org/10.3790/schm.2024.380533.

2

Origins

Abstract This chapter describes the early history of the English noun "liberal," which entered the English language from Spain in the 1810s. The Spanish *liberales* supported the Constitution of 1812, which was republican in spirit. So the word "liberals" came to refer in England to those who supported constitutionalist and republican movements abroad. The word "liberals" then came to refer to a pro-reform clique in the Tory ministry of Lord Liverpool; and then to political reformers in Parliament more generally; and then to a parliamentary coalition of Whigs, Radicals, Repealers, and Reformers.

Keywords Nineteenth-century British liberals · British liberal party history · Elie Halevy · George Canning · Spanish *liberales*

According to Elie Halevy, the great French historian of nineteenth-century British politics, the English noun "liberal," denoting a member of a political party, comes from the Spanish word *liberales*, which

P. de Marneffe, *The Myth of Classical Liberalism*, Palgrave Studies in Classical Liberalism,
https://doi.org/10.1007/978-3-032-14319-8_2

referred to members of the constitutional party formed during the Spanish War of Independence, 1808–1814.[1] Although the details of Halevy's story are open to question, as explained below, it is now commonly accepted that the English noun derives from the Spanish.[2] Here is the backstory.

In March 1808, King Charles IV of Spain abdicated in favor of his son Ferdinand, after a palace riot forced the removal of Charles's

[1] Elie Halevy, *The Liberal Awakening, 1815–1830*, trans. E.I. Watkin (New York: Peter Smith, 1949), 81.

[2] See, for example, Duncan Bell, "What is Liberalism?" *Political Theory* 42, no. 6 (2014): 682–715; Alan Bullock and Maurice Shock, *The Liberal Tradition from Fox to Keynes* (New York: New York University Press, 1957); J.C.D. Clark, *English Society 1660–1832* (New York: Cambridge University Press, 2000); Edmund Fawcett, *Liberalism: The Life of an Idea*, 2nd ed. (Princeton, NJ: Princeton University Press, 2018); Michael Freeden, *Liberalism: A Very Short Introduction* (New York: Oxford University Press, 2015); Raymond Geuss, *History and Illusion in Politics* (New York: Cambridge University Press, 2001); David Haury, *The Origins of the Liberal Party and Liberal Imperialism* (New York: Garland Publishing, 1987); Daisy Hay, "Liberals, *Liberales*, and *The Liberal*: A Reassessment," *European Romantic Review* 19 (2008): 307–20; Maurizio Isabella, *Risorgimento in Exile* (New York: Oxford University Press, 2009); Jorn Leonhard, "From European Liberalism to the Languages of Liberalisms: The Semantics of 'Liberalism' in European Comparison," *Redescriptions: Yearbook of Political Thought and Conceptual History* 8 (2004): 17–51; Thomas P. Neill, *The Rise and Decline of Liberalism* (Milwaukee, WI: Bruce Publishing, 1953); R.R. Palmer, Joel Colton and Lloyd Kramer, *History of the Modern World: Since* 1815 (New York: McGraw Hill, 2007); Jonathan Parry, *The Rise and Fall of Liberal Government in Victorian Britain* (New Haven, CT: Yale University Press, 1993); Ronald Rotunda, *The Politics of Language: Liberalism as Word and Symbol* (Iowa City, IA: University of Iowa Press, 1986); J. Salwyn Schapiro, *Liberalism: Its Meaning and History* (Princeton, NY: Van Nostrand, 1958); George H. Smith, *The System of Liberty: Themes in the History of Classical Liberalism* (New York: Cambridge University Press, 2013); Arthur Thomson, "'Liberal': Nagra anteckningar till ordets historia," in *Festschrifft tillagnad Theodor Hjelmquist pa sextiarsdagen den 11 April 1926* (Lund, Sweden: Karl Bloms Boktryckeri, 1926); Eric Voegelin, "Liberalism and Its History," trans. Mary Algozin and Keith Algozin, *Review of Politics* 36, no. 4 (1974): 504–20. In 1889 Auguste Nefftzer maintained that that the word "liberals," referring to a political party, was first used in France in the early years of the nineteenth century, but he provides no documentation. See Auguste Nefftzer, "Liberalism," in *Cyclopedia of Political Science, Political Economy, and of the Political History of the United States*, vol. 2, ed. John Joseph Lalor (New York: Maynard, Merrill, 1889), 764–65. Possibly Nefftzer was relying on an 1823 *Blackwood's* article suggesting that the term "Liberals" was "imported" from France. See R.S., "The Candid. No. I," *Blackwood's Edinburgh Magazine* 12 (1823), 110. Helena Rosenblatt writes that there was a group in Sweden around 1809 who called itself "the liberal party," who were "influenced by French revolutionary ideas and who advocated principles such as equality before the law, constitutional and representative government, and freedom of the press, conscience and trade," and who were also known as "the liberal side" or "the liberals." But she presents no reason to believe that anyone in England was aware of this party or its name. See Helena Rosenblatt, *The Lost History of Liberalism* (Princeton, NJ: Princeton University Press, 2018), 61–2.

unpopular chief minister, Manuel Godoy. With 100,000 French troops in Spain—ostensibly there to fight with Spain against England—Napoleon pressured Ferdinand to abdicate back in favor of his father, Charles, and then pressured Charles to abdicate in favor of Napoleon's brother, Joseph. Against this national humiliation, the Spanish rose up and, with Charles and Ferdinand under house arrest in France, local notables formed *juntas*—administrative councils—to organize armed resistance to the French and to administer local affairs. Members of town juntas were chosen by popular election; town juntas sent representatives to provincial juntas, and provincial juntas sent representatives to a Supreme Central Junta. When Napoleon crossed the Pyrenees to crush the Spanish resistance and occupy Madrid, the Junta Central fled to Seville and then to Cadiz, where its successor, the Regency of Five, established a *cortes*, or parliament. Over the next two years, representatives from Spain and Spanish America were elected to this cortes, which first convened in September 1810.

In 1812, the Cortes Generales promulgated a new constitution that was republican in spirit. Although it recognized Ferdinand as the legitimate monarch of Spain, it sharply limited his legal authority. It endorsed the republican doctrine of popular sovereignty, that sovereignty "belongs" to "the people" and not to the king. It established a representative government. It provided a mechanism through which laws could be enacted without the king's consent. It prohibited the king from dissolving the Cortes or preventing it from meeting. It sharply limited the king's discretionary authority in foreign and domestic affairs. It created only a single legislative chamber, and no second chamber, such as the House of Lords, to represent the interests of the nobility and the Catholic Church. And it created a framework for eliminating the traditional judicial authority of the landed aristocracy.

Those who supported this new constitution came to be known as *liberales*—the liberal ones—and those who opposed it came to be known as *serviles*—the servile ones. The *serviles* were "legitimists" who favored a return to "absolutism"—a monarchy unbounded by a constitution; they rejected the principle of popular sovereignty, holding instead that sovereignty resides in the monarch; and they opposed the extreme degree to which the Constitution of 1812 limited the monarch's executive authority.

Traveling in Spain in 1813, after the Constitution of 1812 had been promulgated, a 20-year old Lord John Russell wrote from Madrid to his friend and mentor Lord Holland:

> I never saw so fine a people as this. They are anxious for the Cortes to come here, and I hope to God they may, for the spirit of this town is the only thing that can check the folly of the liberales. These people have now gained a complete victory over the serviles and they want to put in practice all their foolish notions of Republick. Their folly and ignorance have turned the whole country against the Cortes.[3]

This passage shows that in 1813, English speakers were aware of the opposition between the *liberales* and *serviles* in Spain and that they identified the *liberales* with republicanism.

After Wellington defeated the French army in Spain in 1814, Joseph abdicated the Spanish throne and Napoleon released Ferdinand to return to his homeland. With the support of the Spanish army, Ferdinand then promptly repudiated the Constitution of 1812 and started having *liberales* arrested. The earliest use of the English word "Liberals" identified by the *Oxford English Dictionary*[4] is in an 1814 article on this episode in *The Leeds Mercury*.

> Every day furnishes new proofs of the unpopularity of Ferdinand, and the instability of his Government.—Weak and offensive must be that Sovereign under whom public men will refuse to accept honours and office—and such is the state of Ferdinand. He has nominated a Commission to try the Members of the Cortes, called in derision the *Liberals*, (for liberal sentiments are a crime in his eyes) now in prison, but two of the Judges have sent in their resignation.[5]

---

[3] John Prest, *Lord John Russell* (London: Macmillan, 1972), 14.

[4] *Oxford English Dictionary*, s.v. "liberal (n.), sense 3.a," June 2024, https://doi.org/10.1093/OED/1114402603.

[5] Report on the arrest of Liberals in Spain, *Leeds Mercury*, October 8, 1814, 3.

Here, the English word "Liberals" refers to members of a *Spanish* political party, not to an English one. So, when did the English word "Liberals" first refer to members of an *English* political party?

Halevy writes:

> . . . it was the Spanish democrats who introduced into the political vocabulary of England, indeed of the whole of Europe, a new word. In opposition to the "serviles", the partisans of absolute monarchy, they [the Spanish democrats] called themselves the "Liberales." It then became the habit among Tory polemical writers to dub the more thoroughgoing members of the Whig Opposition "Liberales", Liberals, that is to say, partisans of liberty after the pattern of Cadiz. In the long run the epithet was accepted by those against whom it had been directed until it finally became the official designation of the revived and reconstituted Whigs.[6]

Although this story has been repeated in various forms,[7] it warrants more scrutiny than it commonly receives.

Halevy writes that "*Liberales*" is what the Spanish constitutionalists "called themselves," but he provides no documentation, which is noteworthy because a party name is sometimes created by its opponents, as Halevy recognizes, and it is hard to believe that the *serviles* came up with *this* name for themselves—one historian writes that this is how they were "scornfully known by the liberals."[8] Furthermore, according to *The*

---

[6] Halevy, *Liberal Awakening*, 81.

[7] See, for example, Samuel H. Beer, "Liberalism and the National Idea," in *Left, Right, and Center: Essays on Liberalism and Conservativism in the United States*, ed. Robert A. Goldwin (Chicago: Rand McNally, 1965); Bell, "What Is Liberalism?"; Fawcett, *Liberalism*; Haury, *Origins of the Liberal Party;* T.A. Jenkins, *The Liberal Ascendency, 1830–1886* (Basingstroke: Macmillan, 1994); Jorn Leonhard, "'*An odious but intelligible phrase*' ... Liberal im politischen Diskurs Deutschlands und Englands bis 1820–1832," *Jarhbuch zur Liberalismus-Forschung* (1996): 11–41; Leonhard, "From European Liberalism to the Languages of Liberalisms"; Jorn Leonhard, "Conceptual History: The Comparative Dimension," in *Conceptual History in European Space*, ed. Willibald Steinmetz, Michael Freeden, and Javier Fernandez-Sebastian (New York: Berghan, 2017); James A. H. Murray, *A New English Dictionary on Historical Principles*, vol. 6 (Oxford: Clarendon Press, 1928); Neill, *The Rise and Decline of Liberalism*; *Oxford English Dictionary*, s.v. "liberal (n.), sense 3.b," June 2024, https://doi.org/10.1093/OED/4142234098; Parry, *Rise and Fall of Liberal Government*; Rotunda, *The Politics of Language*; Smith, *System of Liberty*; Raymond Williams, *Keywords: A Vocabulary of Culture and Society*, revised ed. (New York: Oxford University Press, 1983).

[8] Charles J. Esdaile, *Spain in the Liberal Age* (Oxford: Blackwell, 2000), 35.

Leeds Mercury report (just quoted), Ferdinand called the members of the Spanish constitutional party "liberals" "in derision," which suggests this term might have been coined by the *serviles*, not the *liberales*. Spanish constitutionalists, such as Agustín Arguëlles, frequently referred to the Constitution of 1812 as "a liberal constitution."[9] So it is not surprising that the Spanish constitutionalists would come to be known as *liberales*. But looking through the record of constitutional debates (*Diario de Sesiones* 1810–1813), I have been unable to find any reference by a defender of the constitution, such as Arguëlles, to his own group as "liberales." Why, then, should we suppose that "liberales" is what the Spanish constitutionalists "called themselves"? There is indirect evidence. Joseph Blanco White, a Spanish émigré who frequented Holland House (a Whig gathering place), edited and wrote political commentary for a Spanish language periodical in England entitled *El Español*. In the August 1812 issue, five months after the Constitution of 1812 had been promulgated, he wrote: "The leaders of the party that has achieved this miserable triumph swell with pride at the title of liberals they have taken on"[10] and in an 1814 issue, he used the phrases "those who called themselves liberals"[11] and "those who call themselves serviles."[12] Although Halevy does not cite these passages from *El Español*,

---

[9] See, for example, Sr. Arguëlles, speech, *Diario de Sesiones de las Cortes Generales y Extraordinarias, 1810–1813*, January 8, 1811, No. 105, 329; Sr. Arguëlles, speech, *Diario de Sesiones*, February 13, 1811, No. 140, 542; Sr. Leiva, speech, *Diario de Sesiones*, September 6, 1811, No. 339, 1786; Sr. Bahamonde, speech, *Diario de Sesiones*, January 26, 1812, No. 479, 2695; Sr. Mendiola, speech, *Diario de Sesiones* March 16, 1812, No. 522, 2929; Sr. Salazar, speech, *Diario de Sesiones* March 25, 1812, No. 531, 2974; Report of the Subalterns, *Diario de Sesiones*, March 30, 1812, No. 533, 2983; Sr. Gordillo, speech, *Diario de Sesiones*, May 6, 1812, No. 560, 3164; *Diario de Sesiones*, September 1, 1812, No. 646, 3625; Sr. Alonso y Lopez, speech, *Diario de Sesiones*, October 9, 1812, No. 675, 3795; Convent of Agustín, statement, *Diario de Sesiones*, October 27, 1812, No. 688, 3886; anonymous statement, *Diario de Sesiones*, December 19, 1812, No. 726, 4137; anonymous statement, *Diario de Sesiones*, March 19, 1813, No. 799, 4848; Sr. Dou, speech, *Diario de Sesiones*, March 26, 1813, No. 806, 4894; statement by governor of Segovia, *Diario de Sesiones*, May 14, 1813, No. 852, 5259; anonymous statement, *Diario de Sesiones*, May 15, 1813, No. 853, 5279, 5280; anonymous statement, *Diario de Sesiones*, July 23, 1813, No. 920, 5779; anonymous statement, *Diario de Sesiones*, August 12, 1813, No. 949, 5928.

[10] "Reply to the Second Letter from an American to *El Español* in London," *El Español* 28 (August 30, 1812), 277.

[11] "Closing Remarks," *El Español*, May and June 1814, 299.

[12] "Closing Remarks," *El Español*, May and June 1814, 303.

he might have relied on them in reporting that *liberales* is what the Spanish constitutionalists "called themselves."

Halevy also does not document a "habit" among Tory polemicists of using the term "liberals" in a disparaging way. This would require identifying a pattern with many instances, and here, Halevy identifies only three instances, all from August 1819, and he identifies them only indirectly. He writes that "liberal" was "employed for the first time as the designation of an English party by *The Courier* in August 1819"[13] and the term is used in three *Courier* articles that month, with two different spellings. Although Halevy does not identify the author of these articles as a "Tory polemical writer," this would be an accurate description.[14] There is no byline, and

---

[13] Halevy, *Liberal Awakening,* 82n3. Rotunda's assertion, *Politics of Language,* 32, is therefore incorrect that "'liberal' in the political sense did not even appear in the English language until 1830."

[14] These three articles were written in response to the so-called "Peterloo Massacre," which took place on August 16, 1819. At that time only about eleven percent of Englishmen had the vote and relatively few of them voted in the industrial northern towns. On August 16, 1819, around 60,000 people met on St. Peter's Field in Manchester to demand greater political representation, specifically universal manhood suffrage. When the yeomen cavalry rode into the demonstration to restore order, hundreds were injured and eighteen died, resulting in what came to be known as the "Peterloo Massacre." Commenting on this event a few days later, the Manchester *Courier* wrote:

> As we predicted, the *liberals* [italics in the original] are beginning to ring their doleful charges upon the transactions that occurred at Manchester on Monday. They lament those transactions, not as growing out of a sad necessity produced by crime and delusion, for in that sentiment every Englishman, worthy of the name, would participate; but as a calamity produced chiefly, if not entirely, by the precipitate zeal of the loyal. This is the way in which they think it their duty to support the government and the constitution in this alarming crisis (*The Courier,* August 19, 1819, 3).

Those here identified as "liberals" are those who are sympathetic with the political aims of the demonstration—greater parliamentary representation. A week later, *The Courier* wrote:

> The *liberals* [italics in the original], of course, attribute this peaceable and orderly conduct [the gathering on St. Peter's Field the previous week] to the lamb-like and gentle dispositions of the Reformers themselves. Yes—We have had some notable instances, lately, (Macclesfield to wit) of their amiable propensities, when not over-awed by the array of civil and military preparation (*The Courier,* August 26, 1819, 3).

Four days later *The Courier* wrote:

> We have too high a respect for the noble qualities of British jurisprudence, to imitate our *liberels* [sic, italics in the original] by prejudging his case, on either side. We will not seek to inflame his judges, because they are industrious to calumniate his prosecutors (*The Courier,* August 30, 1819, 3).

the tone and writing style in the three articles are similar. So all three might have been written by the same person. Three articles written in the same month by one Tory polemicist does not document a "habit among Tory polemical writers." The *Oxford English Dictionary* identifies a similar polemical usage a month later in another newspaper[15] and three years earlier, Robert Southey, another Tory polemicist, had used the Spanish word "Liberales" to refer disparagingly to some Whig politicians.[16] But, again, five disparaging uses in five articles by three Tory polemicists in three years does not establish "a habit."

More importantly, Halevy provides no evidence that those Englishmen who came to identify themselves as "liberals" were the same persons as those against whom this epithet was originally directed by Tory polemicists. The term came into general use as a self-identifier only in the 1830s, and there is no reason to assume that those who came to use it then were aware of how it was used by a few Tory polemicists in the 1810s or that they were responding to this usage. Furthermore, as explained below, the

---

[15] *Oxford English Dictionary*, s.v. "liberal (n.), sense 3.b," June 2024, https://doi.org/10.1093/OED/4142234098. Here is a longer passage which provides context:

> In the interval between the commencement of the poll and the conclusion, the popular frenzy, or, in the language of the *Liberals* [italics in the original], synonimous [sic] with Radicals, the popular zeal could not be restrained: disappointed and enraged at the trick (as the free men said) to deprive them of the exercise of their rights and privileges, they assailed the hustings, compelled the Sheriff to quit them, seized on and destroyed the poll books, extinguished the lights, broke some of the branches from the brass chandelier which lights their hall, and many of the windows of the same edifice, and even threatened to pull it down, many exclaiming, that "if their chief Magistrate could be chosen in a parlor the hall was useless to them" (*The Times*, September 20, 1819, 3, col. 2).

This passage identifies "Liberals" and "Radicals" and suggests, as did the *Courier* articles, that "Liberals" are those who are tolerant of rioting in the service of democratic goals.

[16] The Alien Act gave the government authority to control immigration and to monitor the activities of foreigners in England, so as to control the immigration and monitor the activities of continental revolutionaries. But its continuing validity required Parliament to reapprove the act every year and some Whigs and Radicals opposed the continuation of this law on the ground that continental immigrants posed no threat either to British stability or to the continental monarchies, and because they objected to the English government doing the bidding of continental despots. In 1816, Robert Southey, Poet Laureate and Tory polemicist, referred to those who opposed renewing the Alien Act as "the British Liberales" to indicate that they were overly sympathetic with the continental republicans. See Robert Southey, "Review of *Memoires de Madame la Marquise de la Roche Jaquelein, ecrits par elle-meme*," *Quarterly Review* 15 (1816), 69.

term appears to have been first applied by a member of Parliament to himself, not by a Whig, as Halevy suggests, but by a Tory, George Canning.[17] Finally, Halevy's statement in the above passage that "Liberal" "became [in the 1860s] the official designation of the revived and reconstituted Whigs" must be handled with care, as explained below.

Whether or not the term "liberals" originated with Tory polemicists, we have still to determine when the term was first used by someone to identify himself without intending mockery or discredit. The first example identified by the *Oxford English Dictionary*[18] is the title of Leigh Hunt's short-lived literary periodical, *The Liberal: Verse and Prose from the South,* and a passage in the preface to the first issue explains the meaning of the term in the title:

> We wish the title of our work to be taken in its largest acceptation, old as well as new,—but always in the same spirit of admiring and assisting, rather than professing. All that we mean is, that we are advocates of every species of liberal knowledge, and that, by a natural consequence in these times, we go the full length in matters of opinion with large bodies of men who are called LIBERALS.[19]

Because the "large bodies of men who are called Liberals" at this time were the constitutionalists of Europe and South America who opposed absolute monarchy and advocated representative government, this appears to be the political meaning of "liberal" in the title.[20] This

---

[17] Henry Slesser, *A History of the Liberal Party* (New York: Hutchinson & Co., 1944), 53, describes Canning as "one of the most potent of the progressive Tories."

[18] *Oxford English Dictionary*, s.v. "liberal (n.), sense 3.b," June 2024, https://doi.org/10.1093/OED/4142234098.

[19] *The Liberal (Verse and Prose from the South)* 1 (1822), ix.

[20] An 1821 newspaper article cited by Halevy, *Liberal Awakening*, 128n, provides supporting context for the phrase "large bodies of men who are called Liberals":

> 'Let us coast the European continent from Stockholm downwards. Sweden has a representative government; Norway, the same; in England, according to a foreign secretary, 'freedom is only a habit'; Flanders has a constitution by solemn compact; Spain is almost unanimous in the love, and now safe, we trust, in the possession, of her liberty; Portugal, Piedmont, Naples, three-fourths of Europe, are actually free—three-fourths of Europe are in that grand and proud condition in which the remaining fourth has attempted to proscribe as rebels to its supreme and self-constituted authority' (*The Times* (London), March 17, 1821).

interpretation is supported, too, by another passage in the preface: "God defend us from the morality of slaves and turncoats, and from the legitimacy of half a dozen lawless old gentlemen, to whom, it seems, human nature is an estate in fee."[21] The "half a dozen lawless old gentlemen" presumably refers to the absolute monarchs of Europe, known then as "legitimists" who were "lawless" because not bound by a constitution and who, because they were lawless in this way, seemed (to the author) to treat their subjects as their own personal property. Which "half dozen" monarchs the author has in mind is not specified. Because England, France, and Spain were constitutional monarchies in 1822, perhaps he is referring to the monarchs of Prussia, Austria, and Russia, the Ottoman Sultan, King Ferdinand I of the Kingdom of the Two Sicilies, and the Pope. Or perhaps he is referring carelessly to the monarchs of France, Spain, and England, along with those of Prussia, Austria, and Russia.[22] Although the author is not identified, a review article attributes the preface to Lord Byron[23] and Byron was not always careful in his characterizations of political opponents.

A reviewer of *The Liberal* challenged the aptness of its title, and this might be the first time in history that one self-identified liberal challenged this self-ascription by another. But the specific disagreement here is about who is entitled to view themselves as generous and open-minded, which is not directly relevant to the political meaning of "liberal" conveyed by the title. "We profess to be '*Liberals*,'" the reviewer writes, "but we must claim the indulgence of explaining what *we* mean by liberality," which is "exercising a perfect freedom of thought and opinion ourselves, and *in allowing an equal freedom to other men*. We imagine liberality to consist in putting the most favorable interpretation upon their actions, and the most charitable construction on their motives."[24] This, the reviewer observes, Byron does not do.

---

21 *The Liberal*, vi–vii.

22 A hostile reviewer in *Blackwood's Edinburgh Magazine* assumes that Byron is referring here to King George IV of England as one of the "half a dozen lawless old gentlemen." See R.S., "The Candid. No. 1," 113.

23 "On Liberality," *The Council of Ten* 2 (1822), 152.

24 "On Liberality," 150.

The title of *The Liberal* refers primarily to men of letters, such as Byron and Hunt, who were not, at that time, actively involved in parliamentary politics. The preface nonetheless illuminates how the word was currently understood in its political sense.[25] It does not, however, tell us when an active politician first ascribed this term to himself. The first reference by a member of Parliament to himself as "liberal" that I have been able to find was by George Canning, leader of the House of Commons in the Tory ministry of Lord Liverpool. To understand what he meant by it, more historical background is needed.

After the Spanish Constitution of 1812 had been restored by a military coup in 1820, King Ferdinand called for military support from his fellow "legitimists"—those supporting absolute monarchy. But when France, Prussia, Austria, and Russia tried to get England to go along, Canning, who was foreign minister in 1823, made clear that the British government was committed to a principle of neutrality regarding the domestic political arrangements of foreign nations: it would not actively seek to undermine either an absolutist government or a republican government abroad where it was established. This policy of neutrality led both absolutists and constitutionalists in England and Europe to see Canning as a "liberal" and a "radical," meaning a republican sympathizer.

In applying the term "liberal" to himself, Canning was responding jocularly to a House of Commons speech by Sir Benjamin Hobhouse, who himself was reporting the attitudes of continental legitimists toward Canning. Referring to Hobhouse in the third person as "Mr. H.," the House of Commons recorder wrote:

---

[25] Another influential English writer who identified liberalism with constitutionalism in the 1820s was the historian Henry Hallam. In the *Constitutional History of England*, Hallam wrote of the Glorious Revolution: "The Revolution is not to be considered as a mere effort of the nation on a pressing emergency to rescue itself from the violence of a particular monarch [James II]; much less as grounded upon the danger of the Anglican church, its emoluments, and dignities, from the bigotry of a hostile religion [Catholicism]. It was rather the triumph of those principles which, in the language of the present day, are denominated liberal or constitutional, over those of absolute monarchy, or of monarchy not effectually controlled by stated boundaries." See Henry Hallam, *The Constitutional History of England from the Accession of Henry VII to the Death of George II*, vol. 3 (Paris: L. Baudry, 1827), 357–58.

> Elsewhere, however, he (Mr. H.) [speaking] had heard something which was even a great deal more to the right hon. gentleman's [Canning's] credit, for it was the excessive discontent and vexation with him, which was expressed by the under ministers and attendants, and retinue of prince Metternich and count Nesselrode, and all the other gentlemen of the ante-chambers of the allied sovereigns [of Russia, Prussia, Austria, and France]. "Oh," said they, "matters will go poorly with us now in England: the patron of legitimacy [Lord Castlereagh, the previous foreign minister who had recently committed suicide, and who was thought to be "a patron of legitimacy" because he was more conciliatory toward the absolute monarchs on the continent] is no more; and in his place we find a liberal; nay, more, a very radical,"—to which he (Mr. H.) only replied, "I am afraid not quite." (A laugh!) Whether this was what the right hon. gentleman [Canning] would accept in the light of a compliment he knew not; but so, undoubtedly, stood the facts.[26]

Two days later, referring back to this speech by Hobhouse, Canning referred to himself playfully as "the liberal, I beg pardon, to be quite accurate I am afraid I must say, the radical—Foreign Minister of England."[27] Here "liberal" is roughly synonymous with "radical," which is roughly synonymous with "republican." On other occasions Canning expressed sincere sympathy toward constitutional movements on the continent. Three years later, for example, he said in support of the constitutionalists in Portugal, "May God prosper this attempt at constitutional liberty in Portugal!"[28]

The first time Canning referred to himself as *a* liberal might have come in 1824 (it is not clear whether the word is functioning in context as a noun or an adjective). King George IV had written a letter to the Cabinet expressing concern about the decision of the British government

[26] Benjamin Hobhouse, speech, "Negotiations Relative to Spain," *House of Commons Debate*, 28 April 1823, vol. 8, *Hansard 1803–2005*, col. 1345, https://api.parliament.uk/historic-hansard/commons/1823/apr/28/negotiations-relative-to-spain.

[27] George Canning, speech, "Negotiations Relative to Spain," *House of Commons Debate*, 30 April 1823, vol. 8, *Hansard 1803–2005*, col. 1483, https://api.parliament.uk/historic-hansard/commons/1823/apr/30/negotiations-relative-to-spain#S2V0008P0_18230430_HOC_42.

[28] Howard Temperly, *The Foreign Policy of Canning 1822–1827* (Hamden, CT: Archon Books, 1966), 385.

to recognize the newly independent republics of South America.[29] Observing that the creation of the American republic had fostered the French Revolution, the king worried that the recognition of the Spanish American republics would have a similar effect in spreading republican revolutions across the globe, and he referred to republican revolutionaries as "the Jacobins of the world, now calling themselves the Liberals."[30] Knowing the King's feelings about the recognition of these new republics, Canning wrote to his wife, "that the recognition of the new [South American] states [is] the most distasteful measure of his reign .... It sanctions what he conceives to be a revolutionary principle ... it exposes him to the risk of having a coconut-colored minister to receive at his levee [an official reception]—a circumstance to which I, *liberal* that I am, do not look forward altogether with indifference" (italics in the source).[31]

Those allied with Canning in the Liverpool ministry of the 1820s, such as William Huskisson and Liverpool himself, came to be known by their Tory opponents as "Canningites."[32] They also came to be known as "the liberals."[33] In 1823, Harriet Arbuthnot, wife of Tory politician Charles Arbuthnot, wrote in her diary:

> The evening before, Mr. Arbuthnot was sitting by Mr. Beckett, who said to Mr. Arbuthnot that he was quite sorry to find how much Lord Liverpool had lost the confidence of his staunchest [Tory] supporters by his conduct last session, tampering with the Liberals & giving himself up so completely into Canning's hands.[34]

---

29 Augustus Granville Stapleton, *George Canning and His Times* (London: John W. Parker & Son, 1859), 416–19.

30 Stapleton, *Canning*, 418.

31 Wendy Hinde, *George Canning* (London: Collins, 1973), 369.

32 See, for example, the entry for March 24, 1828 in Harriet Arbuthnot, *The Journal of Mrs. Arbuthnot 1820–32*, vol. 2, eds. Francis Bamford and the Duke of Wellington (London: Macmillan, 1950), 175.

33 See, for example, the entry for February 11, 1823, in Arbuthnot, *Journals*, vol. 1, 214.

34 Arbuthnot, *Journals*, vol. 1, 214.

The following year, she wrote in her diary that Lord Bathurst, another non-liberal Tory, "says that Lord Liverpool had completely and entirely changed his politics and was become quite **a** liberal."[35] A year later, she wrote:

> The Duke [of Wellington] told us they had a Cabinet two days ago in which Mr. Huskisson was very intemperate & presumptuous. The subject in debate was the Corn Law, which the Liberals want to alter, & they would run the risk of again ruining the agricultural interest in the prosecution of their theory of a free trade; and Mr. Huskisson wants to pledge the government to consider the question next year."[36]

Because Canning was identified by Tory opponents as "a liberal" and seems to have accepted the description with good humor, this seems to be an example of the phenomenon that Halevy mentions: accepting a moniker coined by one's political opponents. The term was also accepted by some of Canning's parliamentary allies, Lord Palmerston, for example, who was a Whig.[37] Contrary, though, to what Halevy suggests, it was not only members of the "Whig opposition" that Tories referred to as "liberals"—and who then accepted the moniker with good humor—it was also *Tory* members of a *Tory* ministry, such as Canning and Huskisson, whom the non-liberal Tories referred to as "liberals."

The first reference to an English "liberal party" that I have come across is in 1821, in a letter from E.M. Ward, an English diplomat in Lisbon, to his chief, Lord Castlereagh, then the foreign minister:

> The [Portuguese] Cortes ... are ... [after the constitutional revolution of 1820] a little afraid of England, and of England only. But they think the Liberal party is so strong amongst us [the English] that the [Tory English] Ministry, however they may love despotism and legitimacy, cannot act against them [the Portuguese constitutionalists].[38]

---

[35] Arbuthnot, *Journals*, vol. 2, 329 (July 19, 1824).

[36] Arbuthnot, *Journals*, vol. 2, 389 (April 20, 1825).

[37] After Canning died in 1827, Palmerston, who had been Secretary of War in Canning's ministry, created a list of "our party," i.e., Canningites, that he titled "Liberals of June, 1828." See David Marcellus Craig, "Tories and the Language of 'Liberalism' in the 1820s," *English Historical Review* 135, no. 576 (2020), 1222.

[38] Robert Stewart Castlereagh, *Memoirs and Correspondence of Viscount Castlereagh*, vol. 12, ed. Charles Vane (London: H. Colburn, 1853), 438, cited in Halevy, *Liberal Awakening*, 82.

In this same letter Ward identifies the constitutional cause as "the Liberal cause."

Five years later, Mrs. Arbuthnot referred to "The liberal party, with Mr. Canning at their head"[39] and not long after this, one member of this "liberal party," Henry Brougham, a Whig, used this term himself. In an 1827 article in the *Edinburgh Review*, Brougham identified himself as a member of a "Liberal Party" in the House of Commons, which consisted of both Whigs and Tories.[40] What defined this party was commitment to several reform policies, which Brougham identified as "Catholic Question—Currency—Free Trade—Judicial Reform—Foreign Policy—South American independence."[41] Brougham wrote this article to defend the Canningite ministry against the charge that it was unprincipled and that it had sacrificed Tory principles only to stay in power. Brougham argues to the contrary that the cabinet is unified by a principled commitment to these reforms.

Given the commitment of "the liberal party" to these reforms, it is not surprising that the term "liberals" came to be roughly synonymous with the term "reformers" in the 1830s,[42] and already in the 1820s, the term "reformers" was used to refer to what would come to be known as "the liberal party." Thus, in 1822, Mrs. Arbuthnot wrote:

> Last night Lord John Russell brought on his motion for a reform in parliament [which, much altered, would finally be enacted in 1832]. The Reformers have very much lowered their tune, they no longer insist on annual parliaments & universal suffrage, they do not even mention triennial parliaments, they chiefly turn their views to obtaining an encrease in the number of county members & disfranchising the rotten boroughs.[43]

Then, in an 1828 entry, Arbuthnot identifies "the liberals" as "the reformers":

---

[39] Arbuthnot, *Journals*, vol. 2, 60 (November 28, 1826).

[40] Henry Brougham, "State of Parties," *Edinburgh Review* 46 (1827), 421.

[41] Brougham, "State of Parties," 428.

[42] Joseph Coohill, *Ideas of the Liberal Party: Perceptions, Agendas and Liberal Politics in the House of Commons, 1832–1852* (Oxford: Wiley-Blackwell, 2011), 60.

[43] Arbuthnot, *Journals*, vol. 1, 159 (April 26, 1822).

> Mr. Peel's fear of the liberals in the H. of Commons gets the better of his judgment and temper .... The Duke, on the other hand, says we ought not to think of *popularity* but ought to legislate upon a principle of *justice* ... but *justice* is the last thing the reformers think of. They want to get members for Manchester & Birmingham, & they don't care by what means.[44]

The Reform Act of 1832 was a major event in British political history. It eliminated seats in the House of Commons from small electoral districts that were controlled by large landowners, and it increased the number of representatives from large industrial towns such as Manchester and Birmingham. It also roughly doubled the total number of eligible voters, so that now roughly one in five adult English males was eligible to vote. In both ways, it increased the representation of the middle class in the House of Commons and so the responsiveness of Parliament to middle-class interests.

Joseph Coohill has shown that in 1835 "Liberal" and "Reformer" were used interchangeably in *Dod Parliamentary Reports* to refer to someone who supported the 1832 reform of Parliament and who was open to further parliamentary reform.[45] Norman Gash gives multiple instances of the term "liberal party" used as a synonym for "reform party" at this same time.[46] A specific example can be found in an electoral report by Joseph Parkes, a Radical political organizer: "It is observable that the Scotch and Irish Reformers are all 'good men and true'—no flinchers. Thus the Liberals will have a gross majority over the Ministerialists of upwards of *one hundred*, say on our lists 106."[47]

Three distinct early nineteenth-century meanings of the English noun "liberals" have now been identified. The word first referred to those sympathetic with constitutionalist or republican political movements abroad, which aimed to limit or eliminate monarchical power. Then it

---

[44] Arbuthnot, *Journals*, vol. 2, 173 (March 21, 1828).

[45] Coohill, *Ideas of the Liberal Party*, 34–5.

[46] Norman Gash, *Reaction and Reconstruction in English Politics, 1832–1852* (Oxford: Oxford University Press, 1965), 165 n.

[47] William Thomas, *The Philosophical Radicals: Nine Studies in Theory and Practice, 1817–1841* (New York: Oxford University Press, 1979), 276, and see 241, 294.

referred to members of the pro-reform clique within the Tory party under the leadership of Liverpool and Canning. Then it came to refer to reformers more generally—those who supported parliamentary and electoral reform.[48] Not long after, a fourth meaning of "liberals" emerged: "liberals" were members of a newly formed "liberal party," which coalesced in 1835 to oppose the newly named Conservative Party of Sir Robert Peel.

Earl Grey, a Whig, had been prime minister from November 1830 to July 1834, during which time the Reform Act of 1832 and the Slavery Abolition Act of 1833 had become law. After Grey resigned, Lord Melbourne, also a Whig, served as prime minister until November 1834, when the Duke of Wellington, a Tory, became prime minister, serving for a month, until Sir Robert Peel became prime minister in December. Peel's party had by this time adopted the official name "Conservative" and in December, in anticipation of the coming general election in January, Peel presented his guiding principles in a speech that became known as the "Tamworth Manifesto."[49] In this speech, Peel made clear that, as leader of the Conservative Party, he was not opposed to all reform. He considered "the Reform Bill [of 1832] a final and irrevocable settlement of a great constitutional question" and he was open in principle to further reforms. Where reform was clearly needed, he would support it. But he was also committed to preserving British institutions—the monarchy, the House of Lords, and the Church of England. He would support reforms that were necessary to secure the long-term health of these institutions or to promote the general welfare, but he would oppose reforms that threatened these institutions.

The Whigs retained a majority in the 1835 election, but they lost seats to Peel's Conservative Party, and in February, Whig leaders met with leaders of the Radicals and the Irish Repealers and agreed—in what is

[48] Jonathan Parry, *Rise and Fall of Liberal Government*, 6, writes that Canning "was primarily responsible for establishing the word 'liberal' as British political currency. He claimed that 'liberal' government meant a willingness to listen to public opinion, and that the result was reduced taxes, a more open commercial policy and the encouragement of constitutional principles abroad." However, Parry does not cite a source where Canning claimed this and he does not establish with primary sources his attribution of "primary responsibility."

[49] Robert Peel, "Address to the Electors of Tamworth," *The Times* (London), 18 December 1834.

known as the Litchfield House Compact—to act together to oppose Peel in the House of Commons. Peel remained prime minister until April, when a Whig ministry was formed by Lord Melbourne, a Whig.

This anti-Peel coalition, which supported the Melbourne ministry, and which came to be known as "the liberal party," contained four different groups: Whigs, Radicals, Repealers, and Reformers. The Whigs were politicians from the old Whig families, such as the Russells and the Greys, and those connected to them by family ties, and those of their parliamentary allies who, for whatever reason, did not identify themselves by one of the other labels. The Radicals were those in favor of "radical reform." The most radical of them advocated what we might now call "democracy": universal suffrage, the secret ballot, annual or triennial parliamentary elections, equally sized electoral districts, and abolition of the House of Lords or its transformation into an elective legislative chamber similar to the U.S. Senate. The Repealers were those in favor of Irish independence and so who supported repeal of the 1801 Act of Union, which made Ireland a part of the United Kingdom. The largest group in this anti-Peel coalition identified themselves as "Reformers."[50] The Reformers supported the Reform Act of 1832, which disenfranchised the rotten boroughs and expanded the electorate to include more middle-class men, and they were open to further electoral reform; but, in contrast to the Radicals, they did not endorse the most radical reforms, such as universal suffrage and abolition of the House of Lords.

This anti-Peel coalition in Parliament came to be known as "the liberal party" and its members came to be known as "liberals." At the same time, however, the term "liberals" was used more narrowly to refer to a subgroup within this coalition—the Reformers—in contrast to the others, as indicated by this 1836 analysis by John Stuart Mill:

> The Whigs, who were a portion of the privileged class, and were under the full influence both of the interests and of the prejudices of that class, at once took up a position hostile to any thorough reform. This position the Liberals of the empire have never chosen to participate

[50] Coohill, *Ideas of the Liberal Party*, 107.

> [sic]. They did not repudiate the Whigs; but as little did they repudiate what the Whigs repudiated. They were neither Whigs nor Radicals; they were Reformers. They had not predetermined how far parliamentary reform should go; but they were disposed to carry it as far as, on trial, should be found necessary for obtaining good government. They were not for the [secret] ballot, or annual parliaments, because the opinion did not generally prevail among them that nothing less would suffice; but they had no prejudice against either, if an extension of the suffrage, with septennial or triennial parliaments, should fail to give them a government of which the pervading spirit should be a regard to the public good.[51]

Jonathan Parry infers from the party affiliation listings of non-Conservative members of Parliament that between 1838 and 1847 the term "liberal" gradually replaced the term "reformer" as the label preferred by most members of the reform party.[52] This supports the view that "a liberal" was understood in the 1830s and 40s to be a reformer, someone in favor of various reforms. Initially, the reform that defined the reform party, more than any other, was electoral reform. So in identifying oneself as a "reformer" and then as a "liberal," one conveyed that one supported the Reform Act of 1832 and further electoral reform as well. But self-identified reformers or liberals supported other reforms too, such as Church and tariff reform.

The Corn Laws, enacted in 1815, had imposed tariffs on imported grains to protect British grain producers from foreign competition after the end of the Napoleonic Wars. By 1825, "Liberals" in Parliament had started to seek their repeal, as observed by Mrs. Arbuthnot in the diary entry quoted above.[53] In 1838 the Anti-Corn Law League was formed; in 1846, the Corn Laws were repealed; and during this period, free trade became a central commitment of the liberal party, which is to say that it was endorsed by the vast majority of self-identified liberals. Coohill

---

[51] John Stuart Mill, "Walsh's Contemporary History (1836)," in *Collected Works of John Stuart Mill*, vol. 6, ed. John M. Robson (Toronto: University of Toronto Press, 1982), 342. For a similar characterization of "the Liberals," written three years earlier, see J.S. Buckingham, *The Parliamentary Review* 1 (London: Simpkin and Marshall, 1833), 30.

[52] Parry, *Rise and Fall of Liberal Government*, 167.

[53] Arbuthnot, *Journals*, vol. 2, 389 (April 20, 1825).

shows that between 1847 and 1852 the number of members of Parliament who identified themselves as "Liberal" more than doubled while the number of those who identified as "Reformer" fell by over a third.[54] So, as the "Liberal" label became more common, those who identified themselves as "Liberal" were increasingly likely to be committed to free trade. This might create the impression that "liberalism" was "originally" or "essentially" a free market philosophy. But free trade was not a defining position for all self-identified liberals in the 1830s, and still in the 1840s some self-identified liberals supported protective tariffs; some even opposed repeal of the Corn Laws.[55]

Not only did some self-identified liberals oppose repeal of the Corn Laws, but some self-identified conservatives also supported repeal, most notably Peel, the leader of the Conservative Party, who was prime minister when the Corn Laws were repealed. Should we say, then, that Peel was "really" "a liberal"? So far as I have been able to discover, Peel never identified himself this way.

In 1820, Peel had characterized the phrase "more liberal" as "odious but intelligible,"[56] and here by "liberal" he seems to have meant "in favor of parliamentary reform," which he then opposed. Peel was not one of the Canningites, also known in the 1820s as "the liberals," because he opposed Catholic Emancipation (until he changed his position and supported it for pragmatic reasons in 1829). But Peel was nonetheless a liberal in one sense: he was a reformer and an effective one. As home secretary in the 1820s, he reorganized the British police, and Parliament adopted his proposed reforms of the criminal law, which vastly reduced the number of capital crimes. Hobhouse referred to Peel

[54] Coohill, *Ideas of the Liberal Party*, 41.

[55] Coohill, *Ideas of the Liberal Party*, 48–51, 53, 173, 177, 179, 181, 183, 186, 191–92, 199–200.

[56] John Wilson Croker, "Mr. Peel to Mr. Croker, 23 March 1820," in *The Correspondence and Diaries of the Late Right Honorable John Wilson Croker*, 2nd ed., vol. 1, ed. Louis J. Jennings (New York: AMS Press, 1972), 170.

as a liberal in 1828,[57] and, 14 years later, Richard Cobden, co-founder, with John Bright, of the Anti-Corn Law League, who was elected to Parliament as a "Radical Liberal,"[58] wrote that Peel was as liberal as Lord John Russell, then the leader of "the liberal party" in the House of Commons.[59] A year later, in an 1843 letter to Peel, Cobden wrote, "There are no substantial lines of demarcation now in the country betwixt the Peelite and the so-called Whig or Liberal party."[60]

The official Liberal Party, which formed in the 1860s, was a coalition of self-identified Whigs, Radicals, Liberals, and "Peelites"—members of the Conservative Party who had supported the abolition of the Corn Laws. The first prime minister of the officially named "Liberal" party, in 1868, was William Ewart Gladstone, who had been a Peel protégé in the Conservative Party. Because the newly formed Liberal Party included "Peelites" it is possible that, had Peel not died from a riding accident in 1850, he would have become a member of the Liberal Party and so a "Liberal" in this sense, which leads one to wonder whether he would have come to identify himself as "a liberal." One cause for doubt is that Russell, for years Peel's opponent in the House of Commons, never fully embraced this label himself. In 1837, Russell was willing to endorse the label of "Reformer,"[61] which is not surprising given that he had crafted and voted for the Reform Act of 1832, but, so far as I have been able to discover, he never identified himself as "a liberal." Asked in 1852 why he didn't refer to himself as a "Conservative-Liberal," he replied, "Whig has the convenience of saying in one syllable what Conservative Liberal says in seven,"[62] and in 1874, he still referred to the Liberal Party as "the Whigs."[63] Assuming, then, that Russell never fully embraced the "liberal" label, though he was a leader of the "liberal party," it is doubtful that

---

[57] In a letter to Francis Place, cited in Haury, *Origins of the Liberal Party*, 84.

[58] David Brown, "The Press," in *The Oxford Handbook of Modern British Political History, 1800–2000*, ed. David Brown, Robert Crowcraft and Gordon Pentland (New York: Oxford University Press, 2018), 154.

[59] John Morley, *The Life of Richard Cobden* (London: T. Fisher Unwin, 1903), 246.

[60] Morley, *Cobden*, 392.

[61] Spencer Walpole, *The Life of Lord John Russell*, vol. 1 (London: Longmans, Green, 1889), 283.

[62] Prest, *Russell*, 350–51.

[63] Donald Southgate, *The Passing of the Whigs, 1832–1886* (London: Macmillan, 1962), 354.

Peel, a leader of the Conservative opposition, would have embraced it. A more fundamental reason to doubt that Peel would have come to identify himself as "a liberal" is that he never accepted the view that government policy is properly guided by "public opinion," a view that Russell and Gladstone both endorsed, and which was, for many, a defining commitment of the nineteenth-century liberal party.[64]

I return now to Halevy's contention that "Liberals" "became the official designation of the revived and reconstituted Whigs" in the 1860s.[65] As explained above, "the liberal party" became in the 1830s the *unofficial* designation of a coalition of Whigs, Radicals, Repealers, and Reformers. For the next 30 years, this liberal party was led in Parliament by Whigs—Melbourne, Palmerston, Russell–but it also included many who did not identify themselves as "Whigs"—Radicals, Repealers, Reformers, and Liberals. Between 1833 and 1852 the number of members of parliament who identified themselves as "Whig" steadily declined, from 194 to 53, while the number who identified themselves as "Liberal" steadily increased, from 2 to 179.[66] For this reason it is more accurate to say that in the 1860s "Liberal" became the official designation of the *liberal* party, not "the Whigs." But Halevy might have been using the term "Whigs" here to refer to what historians now refer to as "the liberal party." If so, his claim is simply that, having been revived and reconstituted after two and a half years of Tory rule, this party—whether we call it "the Whigs" or "the liberal party"—was, in the 1860s, finally officially designated the "Liberal" party.

---

[64] Parry, *Rise and Fall of Liberal Government*, 147, 155–57, 169, 225. Gladstone is quoted as declaring "The principle of liberalism is trust in the people, qualified by prudence" in Andrew Reid, *Why I Am a Liberal, Being the Personal Confessions of Faith by the Best Minds of the Liberal Party* (London: Cassell, 1885), 13.

[65] Halevy, *Liberal Awakening*, 81.

[66] Coohill 2011, 41.

3

'Liberalism'

Abstract This chapter identifies several different meanings of the term "liberalism" in nineteenth-century England and describes a debate that emerged in the 1880s over the correct meaning of this word. In the middle of the century, liberalism was generally understood to be a commitment to reforming English political and social institutions so as to increase the power of "the people." But in the 1880s, Herbert Spencer and others argued that "liberalism" was originally understood to refer to what we would now call "libertarianism": the view that the only proper function of government is to protect persons and property from assault, theft, breach of contract, and fraud. This claim of Spencer and his allies is partly responsible for the myth of classical liberalism, but it is contradicted by the available evidence.

Keywords Nineteenth-century British liberalism · J. S. Mill · James Fitzjames Stephen · Herbert Spencer · Libertarianism

The first use of "liberalism" identified by the *Oxford English Dictionary* occurred in 1816, and it refers, not surprisingly, given the early history

P. de Marneffe, *The Myth of Classical Liberalism*, Palgrave Studies in Classical Liberalism,
https://doi.org/10.1007/978-3-032-14319-8_3

of the English word "liberals," to constitutionalism.[1] Here is the full quote (only part of which is presented in the *OED*):

> We have received letters from Madrid up to the 10th instant, which mention that the same arbitrary and scandalous system of conduct exists on the part of the King [Ferdinand], who, on the 25th December, Christmas-day, and a festival which Christian nations have always consecrated to joy, after hearing mass, condemned fifteen persons accused of the crime of *liberalism*, in the same manner as he had condemned the others, to hard labor, banishment, & c.[2]

Several years later, David Robinson, another Tory polemicist, criticizing Canning's foreign policy of neutrality between monarchical and republican governments abroad, referred to constitutionalism as "Liberalism and Republicanism."[3] The following year, King George IV, in a letter to the Cabinet, referred to the official British policy of tolerating the establishment of republics abroad as "the Liberalism of late adopted by the King's Government."[4] So in its earliest English uses "liberalism" referred to constitutionalism or republicanism, or, at least, to non-opposition to constitutionalism and republicanism abroad.[5] It did not

---

[1] *Oxford English Dictionary*, s.v. "liberalism (n.), sense 1," July 2023, https://doi.org/10.1093/OED/2737910176.

[2] *Morning Chronicle*, January 29, 1816, 1.

[3] David Robinson, "The Liberal System," *Blackwood's Edinburgh Magazine* 16 (1824), 452.

[4] Augustus Granville Stapleton, *George Canning and His Times* (London: John W. Parker & Son, 1859), 417.

[5] Thomas Jefferson used the word in a different way in an 1821 letter to John Adams. Adams had recently proposed an amendment to the Massachusetts constitution to abolish the recognition of religious sects by the state. Referring to this amendment, Jefferson wrote to Adams: "The amendments of which we have as yet heard prove the advance of liberalism in the intervening period; and encourage a hope that the human mind will someday get back to the freedom it enjoyed two thousand years ago. This country, which has given to the world the example of physical liberty [in the form of republican government], owes to it that of moral emancipation also. For, as yet, it is but nominal with us. The inquisition of public opinion overwhelms in practice the freedom asserted by the laws in theory." See Lester J. Cappon, *The Adams-Jefferson Letters* (Chapel Hill, NC: University of North Carolina Press, 1959), 569. Here by "liberalism" Jefferson seems to mean an attitude of open-minded, nondogmatic inquiry of the kind pursued by Socrates, which, he believed, would be advanced by separation of church and state. For this use of "liberalism," see *Oxford English Dictionary*, s.v. "liberalism (n.), sense 2," July 2023, https://doi.org/10.1093/OED/1040417520.

refer to Adam Smith's principles of political economy or to the free market doctrines today associated with "classical liberalism" and libertarianism.

A very different understanding of "liberalism" can be found in an 1831 letter of John Stuart Mill:

> . . . liberalism, which is for making every man his own guide & sovereign master, & letting him think for himself & do exactly as he judges best for himself, giving other men leave to persuade him if they can by evidence, but forbidding him to give way to authority; and still less allowing them to constrain him more than the existence & tolerable security of every man's person and property renders indispensably necessary.[6]

Here, Mill identifies liberalism, not with constitutionalism or republicanism, but with the principle of individual liberty that he advocated nearly three decades later in *On Liberty*.[7]

Three years after the publication of *On Liberty*, in 1862, James Fitzjames Stephen offered yet another characterization of liberalism, equating it with the view that "existing institutions" should be altered so as to increase "popular power."[8] Liberalism, in other words, is the political doctrine that political institutions should be reformed so as to reduce the political influence of the landed aristocracy and to increase the political influence of others (particularly the prosperous, educated middle class, though Stephen does not say so here). And Stephen identifies Lord Byron by name, as the person "who first introduced the words ["liberal" and "liberalism"] in their present sense."

> They came into general use on the Continent during the early part of the present century, and probably the first occasion in which they were

[6] John Stuart Mill to John Sterling, 20 October 1831, in *Collected Works of John Stuart Mill*, vol. 12, ed. Francis E. Mineka (Toronto: University of Toronto Press, 1963), 80. These early characterizations of liberalism do not support Amanda Anderson's recent claim that from the "inception" of liberalism, "liberal thinkers were aware of the tension between the abstract value of liberty and the problem of social and economic equality." See Amanda Anderson, *Bleak Liberalism* (Chicago: University of Chicago Press, 2016), 21.

[7] John Stuart Mill, *On Liberty*, in *Collected Works of John Stuart Mill*, vol. 18, ed. John M. Robson (Toronto: University of Toronto Press, 1977), 236.

[8] James Fitzjames Stephen, "Liberalism," *Cornhill Magazine* 5 (1862), 73.

> brought conspicuously before Englishmen was when Lord Byron and his friends set up the periodical called the *Liberal*, to represent their views, not only in politics, but also in literature and religion. The *Liberal* met with little encouragement, and soon came to an end; but the same reasons which led to the adoption of its title, gave the word wide currency both at home and abroad, and especially on the Continent. Like all other significant party names, it embodied a boast and a reproach. Those who originally adopted it as their title said in effect, "The whole established order of things, political, literary, and religious, is narrow-minded and bigoted. We propose to reconstruct it upon larger and more generous principles; and, as the first step, we mean to break down what already exists."[9]

Stephen's story here is incomplete, as is shown by the texts quoted in the previous chapter. As Stephen suggests, it is likely that British reformers embraced the "liberals" label in the 1830s due to the established meanings of the adjective "liberal" in the early nineteenth century: open-minded, enlightened, tolerant, generous. It is doubtful that members of the reform party would have adopted this name for themselves had it meant instead close-minded, ignorant, bigoted, and stingy. But Stephen fails to mention other important factors in the adoption of this name in England. First, the *liberales* in Europe were, like the British liberals, political reformers. Second, many Britons approved of the reforms the continental *liberales* sought, which would make continental governments more like British constitutional government. Third, the idea of increased representation of the common man seemed right in itself to many Britons and had been sought by British political leaders prior to the Napoleonic Wars. Fourth, the pro-reform clique in the Tory ministry of Lord Liverpool had been called "liberals" by their opponents, and in this way the term had come to refer to non-radical reformers, which is what most self-identified liberals were in the 1830s when "liberal" became a common political self-identifier.

Stephen claims, too, that the words "liberal" and "liberalism" "are not greatly remote in meaning from the words 'democracy' and

[9] Stephen, "Liberalism," 70–1.

'democratic'"[10] and he explains the course by which the word "liberalism" came to mean a commitment to more democratic political institutions as follows:

> The historical reason of the connection between the two [liberalism and democracy] is, that those who first introduced the words ["liberal" and "liberalism"] in their present sense complained of the narrow-mindedness and bigotry of the state of things then existing, and proposed to introduce a higher conception of the ends and means of public life by an appeal to the people at large.[11]

Stephen's identification of liberalism with a commitment to democracy is surely incorrect, however, if we understand democracy to entail universal suffrage. This is because only a minority of the liberal party in England, when he wrote this article, endorsed universal suffrage.[12] What virtually every member of the liberal party believed is that the political influence of the middle class should be increased relative to the political influence of the landed aristocracy. But many of them opposed the extension of the vote to the working class before a program of national education had created an informed working-class electorate. Liberalism was committed to "more democracy" in the loose sense of increasing "the power of the people," but it was not a commitment to democracy in a sense entailing political equality.[13]

Despite this inaccuracy, Stephen was right to identify mid-century British liberalism with the view that the political power of "the people"

---

[10] Stephen, "Liberalism," 73.

[11] Stephen, "Liberalism," 73.

[12] John Vincent writes, "no appreciable section of the parliamentary Liberal Party believed in numerical democracy in the modern sense without serious qualifications." See John Vincent, *The Formation of the British Liberal Party* (New York: Charles Scribner's Sons, 1966), 250. See, too, Jonathan Parry, *The Rise and Fall of Liberal Government in Victorian Britain* (New Haven, CT: Yale University Press, 1993), 282; Henry Slesser, *A History of the Liberal Party* (New York: Hutchinson & Co., 1944, 59); and Donald Southgate, *The Passing of the Whigs, 1832–1886* (London: Macmillan, 1962), 300, 313, 320, 389.

[13] Cass Sunstein has recently identified democracy as one of six things that all liberals believe in. See Cass R. Sunstein, *Liberalism: In Defense of Freedom* (Cambridge, MA: MIT Press, 2025), 1. But Sunstein is not making a historical claim here about what self-identified liberals have always believed. He is expressing that he would not, in 2025, count anyone as a liberal who did not believe in democracy.

should be increased relative to the political power of the landed aristocracy. This view, as much as any other, was shared by everyone in the liberal party between 1832 and 1862, whether they identified themselves as "Whigs," "Radicals," "Repealers," "Reformers," or "Liberals."

Two decades later, however, in the 1880s, a group of self-identified liberals argued that the term "liberalism" originally referred to what political theorists now call "libertarianism": commitment to a general principle of liberty that prohibits the government from limiting individual liberty for any reason other than the prevention of interpersonal injustices, such as murder, assault, theft, breach of contract and fraud, a principle that entails, among other things, that the government may not tax people to fund poverty relief or universal education and that it may not regulate working conditions for reasons of health and safety.[14] In the 1880s, political commentators who endorsed this libertarian view, which they called "individualism,"[15] argued that liberalism, as originally understood, was equivalent to libertarianism; and they argued that those who, in the 1880s, identified themselves as "liberals" and who advocated taxation for poverty relief and universal compulsory education, or who advocated legislation to regulate working conditions, and who claimed that "liberalism" warranted these policies, had lost sight of its original meaning and were misusing the term.

The leading proponent of this libertarian understanding of liberalism was Herbert Spencer. In "The New Toryism," first published in 1884, Spencer distinguished the "so-called liberalism of the present" from "what liberalism was in the past."[16] Liberalism in the past "habitually stood for individual freedom *versus* State-coercion."[17] That is, it held that state coercion should be reduced to the greatest extent possible, limited to protecting individuals from interpersonal wrongs, such as

[14] An influential contemporary version of this view is presented in Robert Nozick, *Anarchy, State, and Utopia* (New York: Basic Books, 1974).

[15] See, for example, Bruce Smith, *Liberty and Liberalism: A Protest against the Growing Tendency toward undue Interference by the State, with Individual Liberty, Private Enterprise and the Rights of Property* (London: Longmans, Green, 1887), 252, 310.

[16] Herbert Spencer, "The New Toryism," in *The Man Versus the State* (Indianapolis, IN: Liberty Fund, 1982), 10.

[17] Spencer, "New Toryism," 10.

murder, assault, theft, breach of contract, and fraud. Present-day "so-called liberalism," Spencer observes, has lost sight of this principle and has endorsed other forms of state coercion, such as compulsory education laws[18] and laws regulating factory conditions and limiting the hours that can be worked by adults in mines and factories.[19] Past liberalism—i.e., libertarianism—is what Spencer identifies as "true liberalism."[20] What passes for liberalism in 1884, Spencer argues, is really nothing but a new form of Toryism, which holds that it is the proper function of government to limit people's liberty for their own good on the assumption that the ruling class knows what's best for them.

A year later, Spencer's understanding of liberalism was endorsed by Edward Dicey, the older brother of legal theorist A.V. Dicey and a first cousin of James Fitzjames Stephen. In 1885, Dicey wrote:

> According to the creed of Liberalism, as I learnt it in bygone days, the cardinal tenet of our faith was the absolute right of the individual to do whatever he thought fit, so long as he did not by his action deprive others of like right. Freedom of thought, freedom of religion, freedom of speech, freedom of writing, freedom of labour, freedom of trade were claimed, and defended upon the general principle, that the State—or, in other words, the majority of the citizens—acted unwisely and unjustly in interfering with any exercise of individual liberty, provided always the liberty so exercised did not infringe the liberties of others. ... *Laissez faire* was our motto, and to that motto I for one still adhere. ... To remove monopolies, to do away with privilege, to throw open employments, to make neither creed, nor birth, nor station a barrier to success, to provide for all men a chance of rising by their own exertions—this, as I understand it, is the mission of true Liberalism, and this mission, as I conceive, is best accomplished by carrying out to the utmost the grand principle of individual freedom.[21]

Dicey goes on to identify laws recently enacted by the Liberal Party in Parliament that are inconsistent with this "grand principle of individual

[18] Spencer, "New Toryism," 19–20.
[19] Spencer, "New Toryism," 17–19.
[20] Spencer, "New Toryism," 26.
[21] Edward Dicey, "The Plea of a Malcontent Liberal," *Fortnightly Review* 44 (1885), 465.

freedom," including legislation "to feed, house, educate, and elevate the poor by state intervention."[22] And like Spencer, Dicey identifies this kind of legislation with old-fashioned Toryism, and also with "Popery" and "Socialism."[23]

Two years later, Bruce Smith presented a history of liberalism that purported "to show that the term 'Liberalism' . . . in its original and true interpretation was synonymous with 'freedom,'"[24] and he made clear that by a commitment to "freedom" he meant commitment to the libertarian doctrine, which he stated as follows:

> Each member of [the political community] should have secured to him the most absolute freedom or liberty; subject only to such limitations as are necessary in order to secure equal freedom or liberty to all other members.[25]

This, he contends, is "the true principle of 'Liberalism'."[26] It is equivalent, too, to Spencer's principle of equal freedom, originally stated in *Social Statics*, first published in 1851, which Spencer understood to permit the government to limit individual liberty only to protect people from interpersonal wrongs.[27]

There is, however, nothing in the historical record to warrant the belief that liberalism was originally understood to refer to libertarianism. Dicey refers to "the creed of Liberalism, as I learnt it in bygone days," and because Dicey was born in 1832, his "bygone days" must have been in the 1840s and 50s. But, as he must have known, there were at this time leading members of "the liberal party," such as Thomas Babington Macauley, who unequivocally rejected libertarianism. In an 1846 speech to the House of Commons on the Ten Hours Bill—a bill to limit the hours that women and young people could work in a factory to ten hours a day—Macauley (who, on at least one occasion, identified himself

---

[22] Dicey, "Plea," 456.

[23] Dicey, "Plea," 466–67.

[24] Smith, *Liberty and Liberalism*, 6.

[25] Smith, *Liberty and Liberalism*, 135–36.

[26] Smith, *Liberty and Liberalism*, 136.

[27] Herbert Spencer, *Social Statics* (London: John Chapman, 1851), 84, 88–9.

as "a Liberal politician"[28]) said: "I hold that, where public health is concerned, and where public morality is concerned, the state may be justified in regulating even the contracts of adults."[29] In this speech Macauley also said:

> I am, I believe, as strongly attached as any member of this House to the principle of free trade, rightly understood. Trade, considered merely as trade, considered merely with reference to the pecuniary interest of the contracting parties, can hardly be too free. But there is a great deal of trade which cannot be considered merely as trade and which affects higher than pecuniary interests.[30]

Further reason to reject the Spencer-Dicey-Smith claim that "liberalism" originally meant libertarianism can be found in *The Book of Liberals*, a satirical book published anonymously in 1849 under the name "Gabriel Goodfellow." In the preface, the author writes that "the term liberal, though generally used to indicate a species . . . is in reality a generic term, comprising all species, from the mildest reformer to the rankest republican."[31] What unifies the members of this genus is that the liberal is one who advocates for "the people" as opposed to those who are not "the people," i.e., the landed aristocracy.[32] This supports Stephen's general characterization of liberalism, discussed above, but it is also incompatible with the view that "liberalism" referred to a single political doctrine. The author goes on to tell a waggish history of "liberals" from Cain (the brother of Abel) to Napoleon. What the author does not do, at any point, is to identify liberalism with libertarianism,

[28] Thomas Babington Macauley, "Exclusion of Judges from the House of Commons (June 1, 1853)" in *The Complete Works of Thomas Babington Macauley: Speeches and Legal Studies* (New York: Sully and Kleinteich, 1900), 547.

[29] Thomas Babington Macauley, "The Ten Hours Bill (May 22, 1846)" in *The Complete Works of Thomas Babington Macauley: Speeches and Legal Studies* (New York: Sully and Kleinteich, 1900), 452.

[30] Macauley, "Ten Hours Bill," 448.

[31] Gabriel Goodfellow, *The Book of Liberals: A Book for Liberals and Anti-Liberals; Being a Looking-Glass for the Former, and an Eye-Glass (or Spy-Glass) for the Latter* (privately published, London, 1849), v. https://books.google.com/books?id=vKpXAAAAcAAJ&printsec=frontcover&source=gbs_ge_summary_r&cad=0#v=onepage&q&f=false.

[32] Goodfellow, *Book of Liberals*, 15–16, and see 266–67.

which shows that at least one acute political observer in Dicey's "bygone days" had no idea that liberalism was identical to libertarianism.

Mill's unusual 1831 statement of liberalism, quoted above, might be taken to support the view that liberalism was originally understood *by Mill* to be equivalent to libertarianism. But there are decisive reasons to reject the supposition that Mill himself understood his principle of liberty in this way. For one thing, as early as 1848, he supported tax-funded universal compulsory education, which Spencer rightly saw as incompatible with libertarianism.[33] For another, although Mill accepts what he calls "the *laisser faire* principle" as a general rule—the principle that the government should not limit individual liberty except to prevent one individual from harming another—in the same place, he recognizes several exceptions to this rule.[34] Finally, although Mill and Spencer were on friendly terms, Mill thought Spencer's views were indefensibly extreme. In an 1863 letter to John Plummer, he wrote, "I agree with you that Mr Herbert Spencer, in his Social Statics, carries his hostility to government agency beyond reasonable bounds."[35]

Three years before the appearance of Spencer's "New Toryism," T.H. Green, the Oxford philosophy professor, published an essay, *Liberal Legislation and Freedom of Contract*, in which he held that properly valuing individual liberty does not entail the kind of unfettered freedom of contract that Spencer advocated.[36] To value individual liberty properly, Green maintained, was to value *positive liberty*, which he understood to consist in having the opportunities necessary to develop fully, intellectually, morally, and spiritually. Green did not in this essay identify himself as "a liberal" and he did not identify his doctrine of positive liberty as a form of "liberalism," but if Spencer had read Green's

---

[33] See John Stuart Mill, *Principles of Political Economy, with Some of Their Applications to Social Philosophy*, vol. 2 (Boston: Charles C. Little and James Brown, 1848), 528–29; Spencer, *Social Statics*, 330.

[34] Mill, *Principles of Political Economy*, vol. 2, 528–49.

[35] John Stuart Mill to John Plummer, 3 October 1863, in *Collected Works of John Stuart Mill*, vol. 15, ed. Francis E. Mineka (Toronto: University of Toronto Press, 1972), 331.

[36] Thomas Hill Green, "Lecture on Liberal Legislation and Freedom of Contract," in *Works of Thomas Hill Green. Vol. III. Miscellanies and Memoir. With a Portrait*, ed. R.L. Nettleship (London: Longmans, Green, 1888), 370–71.

essay, he would have seen it as a fundamental misunderstanding of what it is to value individual liberty properly, and so as a fundamental misunderstanding of liberalism.

Perhaps it was Green's essay that prompted Spencer to write "The New Toryism." Perhaps he was prompted to write it by another recent essay, "A Protest against Whiggery," by George W. E. Russell, Liberal Member of Parliament and grandson of Lord John Russell, published the year before Spencer's "New Toryism."[37] In this essay Russell contrasts "modern liberalism," which he endorses, with "modern Whiggery," which he rejects. Whereas modern liberalism favors the disestablishment of the Church of England, modern Whiggery opposes it.[38] Whereas modern liberalism favors the disestablishment or reform of the House of Lords, modern Whiggery opposes both.[39] Whereas modern liberalism has faith in the political judgment of the people, modern Whiggery does not.[40] Whereas modern liberalism is committed to universal suffrage, modern Whiggery opposes it.[41] Whereas modern Whiggery is characterized by a tendency "to blindly worship an inexact and half understood science like political economy, and to rely on some parrot-like phrase, such as 'freedom of contract,' as though it contained the clue to all social and political perplexities," modern liberalism rejects this tendency.[42] Because no one accepted the principles of political economy more "blindly" than Spencer, Spencer would have thought that Russell's "modern liberalism," in rejecting these principles, and in allowing government interference with freedom of contract, was nothing more than a new form of Toryism. But from Russell's point of view, Spencer's libertarianism was nothing more than "high Whig doctrine," which he saw as a form of "Conservatism":[43]

[37] George W. E. Russell, "A Protest against Whiggery," *Nineteenth Century* 13 (1883): 920–927.

[38] Russell, "Protest against Whiggery," 923–24.

[39] Russell, "Protest against Whiggery," 924–25.

[40] Russell, "Protest against Whiggery," 926.

[41] Russell, "Protest against Whiggery," 926–27.

[42] Russell, "Protest against Whiggery," 925.

[43] Russell, "Protest against Whiggery," 922.

> The high Whig doctrine would limit the functions of the state to the preservation of life and property, and the enforcement of contracts. Modern Liberalism, on the other hand, regarding the state, with Burke, as "the nation in its collective and corporate character," sees in it the one sovereign agent for all moral, material, and social reforms, and recognizes the special duty to deal with questions affecting the food, health, housing, amusement, and culture of the working classes.[44]

R.B. Haldane, another Liberal Member of Parliament, also rejected the libertarian understanding of liberalism, four years after the publication of Spencer's "New Toryism."[45] According to Haldane, "the liberal creed" is commitment to "the radical idea," which is "equality."[46] Commitment to this idea requires, first, "a complete and thoroughgoing system of national education," to be paid for by taxing the middle and upper classes, which will enable persons born into the working classes to become more prosperous;[47] and second, government-funded affordable housing programs along with minimum health and safety standards for rental properties.[48] Haldane maintains that "the liberal party" has always been "the party of progress" and "the party of change," but, he observes, social conditions demand different changes at different times. The function of early liberalism was destructive: to destroy hereditary privilege. Its goal was "the removal of obstacles which used to block the highway of human progress."[49] Now "liberalism has passed from the destructive into the constructive phase of its history," a phase in which it must construct better opportunities for the working-class.[50] The means of this construction, he contends, should be a system of taxation based on the idea that, because the well-off have benefited more from English

[44] Russell, "Protest against Whiggery," 925.

[45] R.B. Haldane, "The Liberal Creed," *The Contemporary Review* 54 (October 1888): 461–474.

[46] Haldane, "Liberal Creed," 465.

[47] Haldane, "Liberal Creed," 470.

[48] Haldane, "Liberal Creed," 471.

[49] Haldane, "Liberal Creed," 463.

[50] Haldane, "Liberal Creed," 463.

civilization, it is fitting that they should contribute more to improving the opportunities of the less well-off.[51]

It is striking that two different English authors in the second half of the 1880s—Dicey and Haldane—authors in the same political world who presumably knew each other—both confidently refer to "the" creed of liberalism, as if there were only one, and say it is two entirely different things. Is there any reason to believe that in the 1880s, the libertarian understanding of liberalism was the more widely accepted one? No. In 1885, Andrew Reid published *Why I Am a Liberal*, a collection of testimonials which clearly demonstrates that in the mid-1880s there was no one understanding of liberalism.[52] In explaining why they were liberals, or in characterizing liberalism, Reid's respondents gave more than ten different answers. The most common answer (nine) is that liberalism is a commitment to the progressive reform of social institutions.[53] The next most common answer (eight) is that liberalism is a commitment to equal justice or to the recognition and protection of equal rights for all.[54] The next two most common answers (five) are (a) that liberalism is a commitment to the greatest happiness of the greatest number[55] and (b) that liberalism is a commitment to full human development (referred to in one entry as "the perfection of men"[56]).[57] Although some of the respondents might have been libertarians and some might have been committed to Haldane's understanding of equality of opportunity, none of the respondents explicitly committed themselves to either view. Hence, the suggestion of both Dicey and Haldane that liberalism is a single creed—the one they endorse—is not only not supported by the prior history of the term; it is also not supported by the

[51] Haldane, "Liberal Creed," 469–70.

[52] Andrew Reid, *Why I Am a Liberal, Being the Personal Confessions of Faith by the Best Minds of the Liberal Party* (London: Cassell, 1885).

[53] Reid, *Why I Am a Liberal*, 19–21, 54, 56, 63, 72–3, 76–7, 80.

[54] Reid, *Why I Am a Liberal*, 16–17, 22, 45, 57, 59, 82, 109.

[55] Reid, *Why I Am a Liberal*, 15, 31, 34, 85, 97.

[56] Reid, *Why I Am a Liberal*, 40.

[57] Reid, *Why I Am a Liberal*, 40–41, 66, 80, 93, 107.

results of Reid's survey, which was taken in the same decade in which Dicey and Haldane wrote their opposing articles.[58]

In 1859, Mill had characterized the political competition between the two parliamentary parties between 1832 and 1846 as a "trial of strength between the Progressive and Stationary forces"[59] and Mill's opposition of the two suggests a distinction between what we might call "the progressive ethos" and "the conservative ethos." The progressive ethos is the attitude that things can always be improved, things can always be better, there are always ways to advance human welfare and individual development more effectively, which will require institutional reform and change. The conservative ethos is that things are quite good the way they are, and further change risks spoiling what we have. For Peel in the 1820s, Parliament functioned well the way it was, and there was no great need of electoral reform. For Spencer in the 1880s, minimal government intervention into the economy was functioning well and would result in greater human welfare over time. The opposing progressive ethos is well expressed by Mill in an 1868 letter:

> I'm not one of those who think that the political progress of England has but one step more to make before reaching its summit, where it may rest and be thankful; that if a man is ready to vote for the disestablishment of the Irish [Anglican] Church he is ready to do all that the staunchest Liberalism can demand of him. ... We do not want men who cast reluctant looks back to the old order of things, nor men whose Liberalism consists chiefly in a warm adherence to the Liberal measures already passed. ... [We want] men whose heart and soul are in the cause of progress, and are animated by that ardor which, in politics as in

[58] George H. Smith, in a recent history of classical liberalism, maintains that if we look at "what liberals themselves had to say" we will be led to the conclusion that "laissez-faire in all spheres, personal, social, and economic, was the fundamental presumption of [nineteenth-century English] liberalism—its default setting, so to speak—and all deviations from this norm stood in need of justification." See George H. Smith, *The System of Liberty: Themes in the History of Classical Liberalism* (New York: Cambridge University Press, 2013), 16. But the only self-identified liberal that Smith cites in support of this view, on the next page, is J. S. Mill, and if we look at Reid's survey of "what liberals themselves had to say," we find no support for Smith's claim.

[59] John Stuart Mill, "Thoughts on Parliamentary Reform," in *Collected Works of John Stuart Mill*, vol. 19, ed. John M. Robson (Toronto: University of Toronto Press, 1977), 5.

> war, kindles the commander to his highest achievements, and makes the army at his command worth twice its numbers.[60]

Given the history of the English words "liberals" and "liberalism," it makes sense to identify liberalism with the progressive ethos. Haldane correctly observes that from the beginning the liberal party had been "the party of progress" and "the party of change."[61] From the beginning, "the liberal party" in England was the reform party, and a reform party is necessarily a party of change. The most common characterization of liberalism in Reid's *Why I Am a Liberal* is that it is a commitment to the progressive reform of social institutions.[62] But if we understand liberalism as a commitment to progressive reform, this still provides no basis for identifying liberalism with a single creed because different people have different ideas of what "progressive reform" involves. In the mid-nineteenth century, Mill thought it involved one thing, Spencer thought it involved another.[63]

Mill identified himself as an "advanced liberal"[64] and identified his advanced liberalism with commitment to the "cause of progress,"[65] but the term "advanced liberal" implies the existence of less advanced liberals. In 1837 Lord John Russell identified himself as a "reformer";[66] in 1841, he commented to his brother, "In all times of popular movement the

---

[60] John Stuart Mill to Edward P. Bouverie, 19 October 1868, in *The Collected Works of John Stuart Mill*, vol. 16, ed. Francis E. Mineka and Dwight N. Lindley (Toronto: University of Toronto Press, 1972), 437.

[61] Haldane, "Liberal Creed," 463, 464.

[62] Reid, *Why I Am a Liberal*, 19–21, 54, 56, 63, 72–3, 76–7, 80.

[63] See, for example, Mill, *Principles of Political Economy*, vol. 2, 528–29, and Spencer, *Social Statics*, 330, 336. Samuel Moyn rightly identifies nineteenth-century (English) liberalism with "optimism about perfectibility and progress." See Samuel Moyn, *Liberalism Against Itself* (New Haven, CT: Yale University Press, 2023) 65, and see 19, 23, 39. On pp. 23, 33, Moyn suggests, too, that libertarianism involves a rejection of these goals, but in a brief discussion of Mill, p. 59, Moyn seems to recognize that someone (e.g., Mill) might be a libertarian *because they believe a libertarian system would best promote human perfectibility and progress over time*. This, I think, was Spencer's view.

[64] See, for example, John Stuart Mill, "Westminster Election of 1865," in *Collected Works of John Stuart Mill*, vol. 28, ed. John M. Robson and Bruce L. Kinzer (Toronto: University of Toronto Press, 1988), 74; and John Stuart Mill, "W.E. Gladstone, 21 July 1866," in *Collected Works of John Stuart Mill*, vol. 28, ed. John M. Robson and Bruce L. Kinzer (Toronto: University of Toronto Press, 1988), 143.

[65] Mill to Bouverie, 440.

[66] John Prest, *Lord John Russell* (London: Macmillan, 1972), 120.

Russells have been on the 'forward' side";[67] and in the 1850s he wrote that "as the Whig party has always been the party of steady progress, that party can never become extinct till no further progress is required."[68] These quotes show that Russell always saw himself as a progressive reformer. But from Mill's point of view, Russell and other Whig leaders, such as Melbourne and Palmerston, moved far too slowly in advancing "the cause of progress."[69] So if "liberalism" is understood to include both the "advanced liberalism" of Mill and the less-advanced liberalism of Russell, it is an error to identify "liberalism" with any particular doctrine or set of policies, even if we identify liberalism with the progressive ethos.

The plural noun "liberals" came into general use as a synonym for reformers. Because different reformers can aim at different reforms, we should expect liberals to be a diverse group. Some will favor radical reform; others will favor moderate reform. Some will advocate universal suffrage; others will advocate expanded suffrage with a property qualification. Some will support disestablishing the Church of England; others will support reforming it so that it serves its national spiritual and educational functions more effectively. Some will support abolishing the House of Lords; others will support reforming it or reducing its legislative authority. Some will favor abolishing protective tariffs; others will favor reducing them. Some will advocate unfettered freedom of contract; others will advocate laws limiting factory hours and regulating factory conditions. Some will hold that education should be left to parents and private charity; others will hold that there should be universal compulsory education funded by taxation. When Spencer, Dicey, and Smith made claims about the nature of "true liberalism," or about liberalism "in its original interpretation," or about "genuine liberal principles," they were using the words for rhetorical effect to advocate for their preferred policies. Their liberalism was no more "true" or "genuine" than the forms of "so-called liberalism" that they rejected.

---

[67] Prest, *Russell*, 73.

[68] Southgate, *Passing of the Whigs*, 238.

[69] Mill to Bouverie, 440.

4

Hayek's History

Abstract This chapter describes the history of liberalism as presented by F. A. Hayek, a major propagator of the myth of classical liberalism. Hayek maintained that liberalism was originally the name for a synthesis of the constitutional principles of the old English Whigs and Adam Smith's principles of political economy, but this is not supported by the history of the English words "liberals" and "liberalism." Daniel Klein has recently published research on the word "liberal" in eighteenth-century Britain that purports to support Hayek's history. But Klein fails to link his story to how the words "liberals" and "liberalism" were understood in nineteenth-century England and so fails to vindicate Hayek's history.

Keywords Classical liberalism · F. A. Hayek · Adam Smith · Daniel Klein

Nearly a century after these 1880s debates in England about the nature of liberalism, Hayek presented a history of liberalism that might seem to support the Spencer-Dicey-Smith origin story. On Hayek's view, English liberalism was a synthesis of two political doctrines: the traditional Whig doctrine of limited constitutional government and the

P. de Marneffe, *The Myth of Classical Liberalism*, Palgrave Studies in Classical Liberalism,
https://doi.org/10.1007/978-3-032-14319-8_4

principles of political economy espoused by Adam Smith and David Ricardo.[1] Because both doctrines warrant limited government interference with individual liberty, Hayek's history might be taken to support what I call the myth of classical liberalism. Furthermore, Hayek's story is plausible on two assumptions which he might have made: first, that "Liberals" was just another name for the Whigs; and second, that it was the Whigs who first embraced the principles of political economy of Smith and Ricardo. Neither assumption is correct, however. First, as explained above, "the liberal party" never included only Whigs; it included Radicals, Repealers, and Reformers, too. Second, it was the Radicals, not the Whigs, who, as a group, accepted the economic principles of Smith and Ricardo, and the Radicals were only one group in what came to be known as "the liberal party." Finally, the Smith-Ricardo principles of political economy were accepted by some Tories as well as by some Whigs; some Whigs were skeptical of these principles as were some Tories; and the most influential early adherents of these principles in Parliament—William Huskisson and Frederick John Robinson—exerted their greatest influence on policy during the Tory ministry of Lord Liverpool, not a Whig ministry.[2]

Hayek supports his understanding of the history of liberalism with a surmise about how the term "liberal" came into general use.

> It is often suggested that the term "liberal" derived from the early nineteenth century Spanish party of the *liberals*. I'm more inclined to believe that it derived from the use of the term by Adam Smith in such

---

[1] F.A. Hayek, "Liberalism," in *New Studies in Philosophy, Politics, Economics and the History of Ideas* (Chicago: University of Chicago Press, 1978), 125. See, too, George H. Smith, *The System of Liberty: Themes in the History of Classical Liberalism* (New York: Cambridge University Press, 2013), 100–01, 149–50, 195–96.

[2] Alan Bullock and Maurice Shock, *The Liberal Tradition from Fox to Keynes* (New York: New York University Press, 1957), xix; Alexander Brady, *William Huskisson and Liberal Reform*, 2nd ed. (London: Frank Cass, 1967), 48–9; Elie Halevy, *The Liberal Awakening, 1815–1830*, trans. E.I. Watkin (New York: Peter Smith, 1949), 114–15, 197, 198; David Robinson, "The Faction," *Blackwood's Edinburgh Magazine* 22, no. 331 (1827), 408–09; Henry Slesser, *A History of the Liberal Party* (New York: Hutchinson & Co., 1944), 54. Halevy, *Liberal Awakening*, ix, writes: "If Adam Smith was a Whig, he was the most skeptical of Whigs; and Fox, the leading Whig at the close of the eighteenth century, was an opponent of his doctrines. It was as the head of a Tory cabinet that Lord Liverpool allied himself with the political economists, and his economic policy was opposed by the great families who constituted the general staff of the Whig forces."

> passages as *Wealth of Nations*, vol. 2, p. 41: "the liberal system of free exportation and free importation"; and vol. 2, p. 216: "allowing every man to pursue his own interest in his own way, upon the liberal plan of equality, liberty, and justice."[3]

Hayek's inclination here is psychologically understandable, given his own ideological orientation, but it provides no objective basis for an alternative history of the English noun "liberal."

What is "often suggested," by Halevy and others, is that the English noun "liberals" derives from the early nineteenth-century party of the Spanish *liberales.* Halevy does not claim that the English adjective "liberal," as it was understood before 1810, had anything to do with the Spanish constitutionalists. So, strictly speaking, there is no inconsistency between what Hayek writes here and Halevy's account. The two accounts are inconsistent, however, if Hayek is suggesting that the *noun* "liberals" came into general usage in England *as a result of* Smith's writings, and, if this is what Hayek was claiming, there are many reasons to reject this conjecture.

First, as explained above, when the noun "liberal" first entered English usage in the 1810s, it was used to refer to constitutionalists and republicans. Second, the group that uniformly embraced Smith's economic principles, such as Ricardo, were known in the 1820s as "radicals," not as "liberals." Third, the self-ascription of Hunt and Byron in the title of their journal *The Liberal* was a reference to their constitutionalism and republicanism and had nothing to do with Smith's principles of political economy. Fourth, the term "liberals" came into common usage in the 1830s as a synonym for "reformers," not as a synonym for "radicals" (at a time when the term "radicals" was understood to refer to those who embraced Ricardo's economic principles and James Mill's principles of government). Fifth, the term "liberals" came to apply to radicals who were disciples of Smith and Ricardo only with the formation of the liberal coalition in the mid-1830s. Sixth, Hayek presents no evidence that those who saw themselves as pro-reform and who increasingly referred to themselves as "liberals" in the

---

[3] F.A. Hayek, *The Constitution of Liberty* (Chicago: University of Chicago Press, 1960), 529n13.

1830s had read Smith's *The Wealth of Nations* or were thinking about it when they started referring to themselves in this way. Seventh, Adam Smith used the term as an adjective, not as a noun, and in the two contexts that Hayek cites, quoted above, the term can be interpreted to mean "free from restraint"[4] or "freely permitted" and "unobstructed"[5] which are not related to the political meaning of "liberal" that emerged in England in the early nineteenth century.

Daniel Klein has recently offered what he takes to be a defense of Hayek's story, arguing that the nouns "liberal" and "liberalism" "stemmed from the political adjective *liberal*, which gets its sustained start in 1769."[6] Klein does not explicitly define the term "political adjective," but he seems to mean that the adjective "liberal" is used to express approval of some government policies and disapproval of others. Klein makes a convincing case that prior to 1769, "liberal" was not commonly used in this way. He also succeeds in showing that from 1769 on, Adam Smith and others did use "liberal" in this way. This, however, does not warrant the conclusion that the noun "liberals," as this word was understood in the 1820s, by Byron or by Canning or by the Tory opponents of the Canning clique, was derived from the political use of this adjective by Smith and others in the eighteenth century, or that "liberalism" as it was understood by members of the "the liberal party" in Parliament from the 1830s onward was derived from it. Furthermore, in all the eighteenth-century contexts that Klein identifies, the adjective "liberal" is plausibly understood to mean one of the following: open-minded, tolerant, permissive, enlightened, or progressive. Although these meanings likely contributed to the adoption of the term by members of the liberal party, they do not on their own explain why the reform party in England adopted the name "liberals." To understand this, we must recognize that "liberals" had an independent meaning,

---

[4] *Oxford English Dictionary*, s.v. "liberal (adj.), sense 3.a," June 2024, https://doi.org/10.1093/OED/8569985106.

[5] *Oxford English Dictionary*, s.v. "liberal (adj.), sense 3.b," June 2024, https://doi.org/10.1093/OED/5983918927.

[6] Daniel Klein, "'Liberal' as a Political Adjective (in English), 1769–1824," *Journal of Contextual Economics—Schmollers Jahrbuch* 143 (2024), 2, https://doi.org/10.3790/schm.2024.380533.

derived from continental politics, referring to constitutionalists and republicans.

The Hayek-Klein story also does not explain why there was no "liberal party" in the early American republic. The explanation suggested in Chap. 1 is this: given that "the liberals" in Europe were those who supported constitutional or republican government, and given that the United States was formed as a constitutional republic, there was no need for a "liberal party" in early nineteenth-century America.[7] In contrast, there was a need for a Smithian/Ricardian free trade party because one of the central political disagreements in the early American republic was over the wisdom and justice of protective tariffs.[8] So if the Hayek/Klein story were correct, the absence of an American "liberal" party in the first half of the nineteenth century would be more puzzling.

Further reason to doubt the Hayek-Klein origin story is provided by John Vincent, who writes:

> The tendency to regard the Liberals as composed of opposed wings of Whigs and Radicals is ... incorrect. The great bulk of the Liberal MP's were neither Whigs nor Radicals but simply commonplace wealthy Englishmen whose political actions were bound neither by affiliation to great houses nor by theoretical intransigence.[9]

Vincent goes on to write, "The [free-trade] Manchester School [of Cobden and Bright] played no part in the formation of the Liberal Party"[10] and John Stuart Mill—regarded by many as the quintessential nineteenth-century liberal—"in the 1840s took no part in the Free Trade agitation."[11] This suggests that Hayek's understanding of the origin of liberalism is based on a post-1846 understanding, when commitment to principles of free trade became an article of faith among a majority of the liberal party. In any case, Hayek's story about the origins of liberalism does not take into account the ways in which "liberalism" was understood

---

[7] A related observation is made in Hayek, "Liberalism," 121.

[8] Douglas A. Irwin, *Clashing Over Commerce* (Chicago: Chicago University Press, 2017).

[9] John Vincent, *The Formation of the British Liberal Party* (New York: Charles Scribner's Sons, 1966), xxxiv-xxxv.

[10] Vincent, *Formation of the British Liberal Party*, 33.

[11] Vincent, *Formation of the British Liberal Party*, 150.

by English-speakers prior to the anti-Corn Law agitation, when it referred, in different contexts, to other commitments: the progressive reform of social institutions, increasing the power of "the people," and support for republican government abroad.

5

"Liberals" in America

Abstract This chapter presents and challenges another element of the myth of classical liberalism, which is that Franklin Roosevelt changed the meaning of the words "liberals" and "liberalism" so that they came to mean the opposite of what they had originally meant. Contrary to what several scholars have implied, the way in which Roosevelt used the terms "liberals" and "liberalism" in the 1930s was already well-established in England in the 1880s and well-established in America in the 1920s. This chapter, too, challenges Hayek's claim that liberalism, as understood in the U.S. after the New Deal, was a radical departure from English liberalism of the nineteenth century.

Keywords Franklin D. Roosevelt · New Deal · Carl Schurz · Liberal Republican party · Herbert Hoover · Robert A. Taft · F.A. Hayek · Ludwig von Mises · Hubert Humphrey

In 1938, President Franklin D. Roosevelt presented the following contrast between "liberalism" and "the conservative school of thought":

P. de Marneffe, *The Myth of Classical Liberalism*, Palgrave Studies in Classical Liberalism,
https://doi.org/10.1007/978-3-032-14319-8_5

> Another indirect accomplishment of this Congress has been its response to the devotion of the American people to a course of sane consistent liberalism. The Congress has understood that under modern conditions government has a continuing responsibility to meet continuing problems, and that government cannot take a holiday of a year, a month, or even a day just because a few people are tired or frightened by the inescapable pace of this modern world in which we live .... Be it clearly understood, however, that when I use the word "liberal," I mean the believer in progressive principles of democratic, representative government and not the wild man who, in effect, leans in the direction of Communism, for that is just as dangerous as Fascism. The opposing or conservative school of thought, as a general proposition, does not recognize the need for government itself to step in and take action to meet these new problems. It believes that individual initiative and private philanthropy will solve them—that we ought to repeal many of the things we have done and go back, for instance, to the old gold standard, or stop all this business of old age pensions and unemployment insurance, or repeal the Securities and Exchange act, or let monopolies thrive unchecked—return, in effect, to the kind of government we had in the twenties.[1]

Here, Roosevelt identified those who supported his New Deal policies as "liberals" and those who opposed his policies as embracers of the "conservative school of thought."

Because liberalism had been understood by some, such as Herbert Spencer, to consist of principled opposition to government intervention into the economy, and the New Deal involved government intervention, some have concluded that Roosevelt changed the meaning of the words "liberal" and "liberalism."

Verlan Lewis writes:

> Famously, Roosevelt utilized the new power of radio to speak directly to the American electorate and explain the reasoning behind his New Deal. He successfully appropriated the term "liberal" to describe his expansion of national government power and economic interventionism—the opposite

[1] Franklin D. Roosevelt, "Fireside Chat on Primaries," June 24, 1938, *The American Presidency Project*, https://www.presidency.ucsb.edu/documents/fireside-chat-14.

of what it had previously meant. By putting familiar terms to new uses, FDR was able to radically change the [Democratic] party's ideology.[2]

Justin Vaïsse writes:

> Roosevelt's New Deal ... marks the beginning of the opposition between "liberalism" in the American sense of the term—a left-wing policy of state intervention—and "liberalism" in the European sense—a right-wing doctrine referring primarily to laisser faire in the economic sphere.[3]

Christopher Ellis and James Stimson write:

> We know the term "liberal" has a very long history, but with a quite different—almost opposite—connotation, support for freedom from government intervention in all matters. So how did a program of activist government intervention in the economy become "liberalism"? Franklin D. Roosevelt is at the center of an answer .... FDR hit upon "liberal" for its positive association with freedom and for its absence of any link with the socialism and communism that were threatening and unpopular in American opinions. And thus a novel term for a belief in activist government involvement in the economy, and activist in particular in support of those most in need, the poor, became part of the American lexicon.[4]

Brian Barry writes:

> As is known, Roosevelt's inner circle of advisors felt that to describe their program as "social democratic" would be imprudent and they therefore appropriated the word "liberal" for it.[5]

Sidney Milkis writes:

> Roosevelt was the first statesman to "appropriate" the term *liberalism* and make it part of the common political vocabulary. In doing so,

---

[2] Verlan Lewis, *Ideas of Power* (New York: Cambridge University Press, 2019), 123.

[3] Justin Vaïsse, *Neoconservativism: The Biography of a Movement*, trans. Arthur Goldhammer (Cambridge, MA: Harvard University Press, 2010), 6.

[4] Christopher Ellis and James A. Stimson, "Symbolic Ideology in the American Electorate," *Electoral Studies* 28, no. 3 (2009), 397.

[5] Brian Barry, *Why Social Justice Matters* (New York: Polity Press, 2005), 6; Barry provides no supporting citation.

> however, he reworked—some claimed perverted—the elements of the old faith into a modern form. Roosevelt pronounced a liberalism that evoked the *Declaration*'s concept of rights, but linked this concept to programmatic expansion.[6]

Seymour Lipset writes:

> Historically, liberalism everywhere has stood for anti-statism, laissez faire . . . . But the term "liberal" changed meaning in America, in some ways into its exact opposite. During the 30s, Franklin D. Roosevelt's New Deal introduced, in Richard Hofstadter's, phrase "a social democratic tinge" into American politics . . . . Roosevelt turned to government planning, economic regulations, support of trade unionism, public ownership and huge welfare programs. It was these programs that came to be identified as Democratic liberalism. In effect, as Mr. Hofstadter implied, liberalism became the American variant of social democracy.[7]

These passages create the impression that before Roosevelt got ahold of the words, "liberalism" referred to libertarianism and "liberals" referred to libertarians. But this is quite false, as shown above. Already in the 1880s, there was a disagreement in England about what liberalism was and who the real liberals were, and some of these Englishmen already understood "liberalism" in roughly the same way that Roosevelt understood it in the 1930s. Moreover, although the nouns "liberals" and "liberalism" were not as common in American political discourse as they had been in late nineteenth-century England, they were in use before the 1930s, and they were used the way Roosevelt used them.

According to one recent account, "it was Roosevelt who introduced the term 'liberal' into popular American discourse,"[8] but the term was already in use in the early 1870s, to refer to members of the short-lived

---

[6] Sidney M. Milkis, *The President and the Parties* (New York: Oxford University Press, 1993), 49.

[7] Seymour Martin Lipset, "Americans Sneer at Liberalism. Why?" *New York Times*, October 28, 1988.

[8] Donald Kinder and Nathan Kalmoe, *Neither Liberal Nor Conservative: Ideological Innocence in the American Public* (Chicago: University of Chicago Press, 2017), 49.

Liberal Republican Party. In 1870, U.S. Senator Carl Schurz of Missouri organized a "Liberal Republican Party" to oppose the nominees of the established Republican Party in Missouri state elections.[9] Success in Missouri led to the formation of a national Liberal Republican Party, which was formed to oppose the reelection of President Grant in 1872. Schurz and his allies had been loyal Republicans. They had supported the election of Lincoln, the Civil War, and the Civil War Amendments. Schurz had served as a general in the Union army. But the Liberal Republicans were at odds with the national Republican party on voting rights for former Confederate soldiers, free trade, and civil service reform.[10] It is not clear why these policy differences led Schurz to identify his group as the "Liberal" Republicans, but the available histories suggest the following speculations.[11]

As a university student in Bonn, Schurz had been active in the movement to make Germany a democratic republic—a representative government without a monarch—and republicans were then known in Europe as "Liberales."[12] So in labeling his American party the "Liberal Republicans" Schurz might have intended to convey that they were the *real* republicans—those truly committed to the republican principle of self-government even as applied to Confederate states. The Liberal Republicans supported the Civil Rights Act of 1866 and the Fourteenth Amendment, but they opposed continued federal government control of the former Confederate states, on the grounds that external control by an occupying military force is incompatible with the republican principle of self-government. Republican government requires representative government; representative government

---

[9] Andrew L. Slap, *The Doom of Reconstruction: The Liberal Republicans in the Civil War Era* (New York: Fordham University Press, 2006), 5.

[10] Slap, *Doom of Reconstruction*, 5.

[11] Alexander Johnston, "Liberal Republican Party," in *Cyclopedia of Political Science, Political Economy, and of the Political History of the United States*, vol. 2, ed. John Joseph Lalor (New York: Maynard, Merrill, 1889); Carl Schurz, *Speeches, Correspondence, and Political Papers of Carl Schurz*, ed. Frederic Bancroft (New York: G.P. Putnam and Sons, 1913); John G. Sproat, *"The Best Men": Liberal Reformers in the Gilded Age* (New York: Oxford University Press, 1968); Hans L. Trefousse, *Carl Schurz: A Biography* (Knoxville, TN: University of Tennessee Press, 1982).

[12] Trefousse, *Schurz*, 14–21.

requires that all segments of society are represented; and this requires that all segments of society have the vote. Excluding some segment of society from voting to protect against unwanted policy outcomes is a mark of monarchical government, not republican government. The Liberal Republicans supported the Fifteenth Amendment and believed that all adult Black males should have the vote on the general principle that all adult males should have the vote, but this same principle, as they saw it, warranted the re-enfranchisement of former Confederate soldiers.[13] So, if Schurz understood "liberalism" as a commitment to republicanism, as it was widely understood in nineteenth-century Europe, this offers an explanation of why he called his break-away party the *liberal* Republicans.

In 1848, Schurz was involved in one of the armed insurrections aimed at establishing a democratic republic in Germany, sometimes referred to collectively as "Germany's liberal revolution."[14] After this revolution failed, Schurz fled, fearing for his life, and ended up in London, with other German political refugees, such as Karl Marx. Living in London from 1850 to 1852, Schurz was likely aware that what was then known as "the liberal party" in England was the free trade party. Because the Liberal Republicans in America were also a free trade party, this suggests another reason why Schurz chose this name for his group.

To pay for the Civil War, the U.S. government had raised tariffs, and by 1870, the average tariff was 47%.[15] In the view of the Liberal Republicans this was far too high, and like some mid-century English liberals, Liberal Republicans regarded free trade, not only as a matter of economic efficiency, but as a requirement of equal justice and equal opportunity, too. English free trade advocates such as Cobden, Bright, and Spencer associated protective tariffs with monopolies, and they associated monopolies with hereditary aristocratic privilege. Their goal in promoting free trade was not only to make markets more efficient and commodities less expensive for the consumer; it was to abolish the

[13] Slap, *Doom of Reconstruction*, 73, 85, 109–10, 113.

[14] See, for example, R. Hinton Thomas, *Liberalism, Nationalism and the German Intellectuals* (Cambridge: Heffer and Sons, 1951), 136.

[15] Douglas A. Irwin, *Clashing Over Commerce* (Chicago: University of Chicago Press, 2017), 222.

system of hereditary privilege which had existed in England since feudal times. Of John Bright, co-founder of the Anti-Corn Law League, John Vincent writes:

> Bright's theory of history and of politics did not derive from any abstract attachment to *laissez-faire* or political economy, or from any construction of his business interests .... The main social problem then was seen as Privilege, privilege existing in some close connection with poverty, no doubt, but still it was Privilege and not poverty that was the central question of Bright's politics. The extreme form of Privilege was "monopoly", whether in the form of an Established Church or of the Corn Laws. The rest of Bright's politics followed coherently from this principle.[16]

The Liberal Republicans of Missouri shared this view of protective tariffs: protective tariffs favored some citizens' economic interests at the expense of others'; they tended to foster and sustain monopolies; and they were fundamentally incompatible with equality before the law and equal opportunity. As Andrew Slap presents the views of the Missouri free traders, "Both slavery and tariffs ... used the power of the state to benefit a special class at the expense of workers. Imposing a tax on workers through a tariff to promote the interests of industrialists was the same, they insisted, as a plantation owner living on the sweat of his slaves."[17] So if Schurz had understood liberalism as a commitment to republican government, and he had seen republican government as incompatible with economic privileges created by law, and he had seen protective tariffs as a form of economic privilege, this offers an additional explanation of why Schurz called his group the *Liberal* Republicans.

While in London Schurz might also have come to regard the English liberal party as the party of good government. Lord Palmerston, a leading member of the liberal party then, was interested in civil service reform.[18] During his tenure as home secretary from 1852–1855,

---

[16] John Vincent, *The Formation of the British Liberal Party* (New York: Charles Scribners' Sons, 1966), 168, 170.

[17] Slap, *Doom of Reconstruction*, 12.

[18] Jonathan Parry, *The Rise and Fall of Liberal Government in Victorian Britain* (New Haven, CT: Yale University Press, 1993), 181.

competitive examinations were introduced for the Indian Civil Service, and the Civil Service Commission was established to certify the fitness of nominees for domestic civil service posts.[19] An admirer of the Prussian civil service,[20] Schurz opposed the American spoils system of awarding government offices to political allies—regardless of competence and honesty—and advocated civil service reform to eliminate this practice. This might have struck him as the same kind of reform that the "liberals" or "reformers" in England had advocated.

Another possible factor is that "the liberals" in England were perceived to be more moderate than "the radicals," and, in supporting the re-enfranchisement of Confederate soldiers and the withdrawal of military occupation, Schurz supported a more moderate policy of reconstruction than the Radical Republicans. Yet another possible factor is that "liberal" was sometimes used to mean "generous" and "magnanimous" and the Liberal Republicans might have seen their attitude toward the South as more generous and magnanimous than that of the Radical Republicans. Generous and magnanimous though it might have been in spirit, the opposition of the Liberal Republicans and others to Radical Reconstruction led to the end of Reconstruction in 1877, which opened the door to systematic violation of the civil and political rights of Black Americans in the states of the former Confederacy.

Because the Liberal Republicans were sometimes referred to in the press as "the Liberals," and might have referred to themselves this way, "Liberals" was recognized as a distinctive partisan identity in nineteenth-century America.[21] The Liberal Republicans were also sometimes

[19] Parry, *Rise and Fall of Liberal Government*, 182.

[20] Trefousse, *Schurz*, 183.

[21] See, for example, "The Proper Time to Agitate for Reform," *The Nation* 14, no. 349 (March 7, 1872), 148; "The Cincinnati Convention," *The Nation* 14, no. 351 (March 21, 1872), 181; "The Week," *The Nation* 14, no. 357 (May 2, 1872), 281; "A 'Political Anomaly,'" *The Nation* 15, no. 366 (July 4, 1872), 5; "Summer Reading," *The Nation* 15, no. 366 (July 4, 1872), 13; "The Absurd Movement," *The Nation* 15, no. 374 (August 29, 1872), 134; "The Week," *The Nation* 15, no. 376 (September 12, 1872), 161; "The Week," *The Nation* 15, no. 377 (September 19, 1872), 177; "The Week," *The Nation* 15, no. 378 (September 26, 1872), 194; "The Week," *The Nation* 15, no. 383 (October 31, 1872), 273; "The Week," *The Nation* 15, no. 384 (November 7, 1872), 290; "What's Next?" *The Nation* 15, no. 387 (November 28, 1872), 343; "The Week,"

referred to as "Reformers,"[22] and as "Reform Liberals,"[23] and as members of a "Liberal Reform movement,"[24] which links the American Liberal Republicans of the 1870s to the English liberals of the 1830s, 1840s, and 1850s. But after Grant won the election of 1872, the Liberal Republican Party vanished, and the word "liberal" did not return to partisan use until the twentieth century.

Although "liberal" was not widely used to refer to a political identity in American political discourse before the 1930s, Americans were divided, from the late nineteenth century on, over the same question of greater or lesser government intervention into the economy that divided English liberals, with those favoring more intervention known in America as "progressives" and "radicals" and those opposed to more intervention known in America as "conservatives," "standpatters," and "reactionaries."

Early twentieth-century American progressives were reformers, as were the British liberals of the 1830s, 1840s, and 1850s. But whereas the mid-nineteenth-century British liberals sought to reduce the economic and political power of the landed aristocracy, early twentieth-century American progressives sought to reduce the economic and political power of large corporations and of the super-rich in order to make it easier for the common (white) man to succeed in business and to influence government policy. They aimed, too, to protect the vulnerable from businesses that had an interest in taking advantage of them. For this reason, the progressives advocated laws regulating factory conditions and limiting factory hours, prohibiting the sale of alcohol, and outlawing brothels.

Writing in 1927, John Dewey recognized a continuity in the reforming spirit from mid-nineteenth-century England to early twentieth-century America and commented on the historical irony that the progressives of his day were battling powerful business interests that had been created by

The Nation 15, no. 388 (December 5, 1872), 358; "The Week," *The Nation* 15, no. 389 (December 12, 1872), 373; "Opening of Congress," *The Nation* 15, no. 389 (December 12, 1872), 381; "The Week," *The Nation* 16, no. 392 (January 2, 1873), 1; "The Congressional Situation," *The Nation* 17, no. 441 (December 11, 1873), 383.

[22] See, for example, "The Week," *The Nation* 14, no. 360 (May 23, 1872), 329.

[23] See, for example, "The Week," *The Nation* 14, no. 357 (May 2, 1872), 281.

[24] See, for example, "The Week," *The Nation* 14, no. 358 (May 9, 1872), 297.

an earlier generation of progressives in the nineteenth century. Reflecting on "the history of the doctrine of Individualism, interpreted to signify a minimum of governmental 'interference' with industry and trade," Dewey wrote:

> At the outset, it [the doctrine of Individualism] was held by "progressives," by those who were protesting against the inherited regime of rules of law and administration. Vested interests, on the contrary, were mainly in favor of the old status. Today the industrial property regime being established, the doctrine is the intellectual bulwark of the standpatter and reactionary. He it is that now wants to be let alone, and who utters the war cry of liberty for private industry, thrift, contract and their pecuniary fruit ... . The irony of history is nowhere more evident than in the reversal of the practical meaning of the term "liberalism" in spite of a literal continuity of theory.[25]

The "continuity of theory" that Dewey refers to here is the progressive idea that institutions must be reformed to reduce political and economic control of the rich in order to create opportunity for others and to promote the welfare of the many, whether the wealth of the rich is created by landed estates, mines, factories, railroads, or banks.

One reason to reject the claim that Roosevelt changed the meanings of the English words "liberals" and "liberalism" during his presidency is that what he meant by these words had been established a half century earlier in Britain. G.W.E. Russell and R.B. Haldane, both Liberal members of parliament in the 1880s, understood "liberalism" to call for a greater role for government in promoting human welfare.[26] Two decades later, Winston Churchill, another Liberal member of parliament, endorsed a similar understanding of liberalism. Commenting on debate about the relative virtues of liberalism and socialism, Churchill offered the following philosophical observation:

> It is not possible to draw a hard-and-fast line between individualism and collectivism. You cannot draw it either in theory or in practice ... .

[25] John Dewey, *The Public and Its Problems* (New York: Henry Holt and Company, 1927), 134.

[26] George W.E. Russell, "A Protest against Whiggery," *Nineteenth Century* 13 (1883): 920–927; R.B. Haldane, "The Liberal Creed," *The Contemporary Review* 54 (October 1888): 461–474.

> No man can be a collectivist alone or an individualist alone. He must be both an individualist and a collectivist. The nature of man is a dual nature. The character of the organisation of human society is dual.[27]

Churchill went on to say:

> I am of the opinion that the state should increasingly assume the position of the reserve employer of labor. I am very sorry we have not got the railways of this country into our hands. We may do something better with the canals, and we are all agreed, everyone in this hall who belongs to the Progressive [i.e. Liberal] Party, that the state must increasingly and earnestly concern itself with the care of the sick and the aged, and, above all, of the children. I look forward to the universal establishment of minimum standards of life and labor, and their progressive elevation as the increasing energies of production may permit. I do not think that liberalism in any circumstances can cut itself off from this fertile field of social effort, and I would recommend you not to be scared in discussing any of these proposals, just because some old woman comes along and tells you they are Socialistic.[28]

Roosevelt's "liberalism" of 1938 is the same as Churchill's "liberalism" of 1906. So clearly, Roosevelt did not change the meaning of the English word.[29]

Years before Roosevelt's presidency, leading English intellectuals, too, had embraced an understanding of liberalism that was consonant with Roosevelt's understanding in the 1930s. Passages from Herbert Louis Samuel, J.A. Hobson, and L.T. Hobhouse indicate the character of this

[27] Winston S. Churchill, *Liberalism and the Social Problem* (New York: Hodder and Stoughton, 1909), 79. From a speech originally delivered in 1906.

[28] Churchill, *Liberalism and the Social Problem*, 81.

[29] Joseph Schumpeter identified 1900 as the time when the phrase "economic liberalism" acquired a different, "almost opposite," meaning. See Joseph Schumpeter, *History of Economic Analysis*, ed. Elizabeth Boody Schumpeter (Oxford: Oxford University Press, 1954), 394. George H. Smith concurs, writing: "In the late nineteenth century, liberals in Europe and America discovered that they were the victims of a linguistic coup. They found that they were no longer regarded as liberals per se but as *old* liberals—a qualification that had been foisted upon them by the self-proclaimed *new* liberals." See George H. Smith, *The System of Liberty: Themes in the History of Classical Liberalism* (New York: Cambridge University Press, 2013), 7.

"new liberalism" and how different it was from the laissez-faire liberalism of Spencer, Dicey, and Smith.[30]

In 1902 Samuel equated liberalism with "one essential doctrine":

> That it is the duty of the State to secure to all its members, and all others whom it can influence, the fullest possible opportunity to lead the best life. When we speak of Progress, we mean by progress the enlargement of this opportunity ... . This stands as the essential principle of the Liberal creed.[31]

Although Samuel does not here use the phrase "equality of opportunity," he identifies a conception of equality of opportunity as "the ideal":

> when in every district there shall be a cheap and thoroughly efficient school for secondary teaching; when every child of exceptional parts, no matter into what class it may have been born, shall have the opportunity of passing by the help of scholarships from the elementary to the higher grade, from there to secondary school, and onward to the university; and when none shall be barred by poverty alone from the best education that the country and age can give.[32]

According to J.A. Hobson, writing in 1909, "The Liberals of this country [England] as a party never committed themselves either to the theory or the policy of ... narrow laissez faire individualism; they never conceived liberty as something limited in quantity, or purely negative in character."[33] He goes on to identify liberalism with a commitment to equality of opportunity,

---

[30] "The New Liberalism" is the title of an 1896 essay by R.B Haldane which quotes with approval T.H. Green's reflections on the value of freedom in Thomas Hill Green, "Liberal Legislation and Freedom of Contract," in *Works of Thomas Hill Green. Vol. III. Miscellanies and Memoir. With a Portrait*, ed. R.L. Nettleship (London: Longmans, Green, 1888). See R.B. Haldane, "The New Liberalism," *The Progressive Review* 1, no. 2 (1896): 133–43. For scholarly discussion of "the new liberalism" as an intellectual movement, see Peter Clarke, *Liberals & Social Democrats* (New York: Cambridge University Press, 1978); Stefan Collini, *Liberalism and Sociology: L.T. Hobhouse and Political Argument in England, 1880–1914* (New York: Cambridge University Press, 1979); Michael Freeden, *The New Liberalism: Ideology and Social Reform* (New York: Oxford University Press, 1978); and Peter Weiler, *The New Liberalism: Liberal Social Theory in Great Britain 1889–1914* (New York: Routledge, 1982).

[31] Herbert Louis Samuel, *Liberalism. An Attempt to State the Principles and Proposals of Contemporary Liberalism in England* (London: Grant Richards, 1902), 4.

[32] Samuel, *Liberalism*, 41–2.

[33] J.A. Hobson, *The Crisis of Liberalism, New Issues of Democracy* (London: P.S. King, 1909), 92.

"which every Englishman requires today in order to secure real liberty of self-development," and he understands equality of opportunity to require equal access to resources—"the right of every man to an equal share with every other in the use of land and of the other natural resources of his native country."[34]

According to L.T. Hobhouse, writing in 1911, "Liberalism is the belief that society can safely be founded on [the] self-directing power of personality"—"that central harmonizing power that makes us capable of directing our own lives."[35] The value of liberty, he goes on to say, "rests not on the claim of A to be let alone by B, but on the duty of B to treat A as a rational being . . . . [F]reedom is only one side of social life. Mutual aid is not less important than mutual forbearance, the theory of collective action no less fundamental than the theory of personal freedom." Moreover, "The 'right to work' and the right to 'a living wage' are just as valid as the rights of personal property."[36] And, finally, "We saw it was the duty of the state to secure the conditions of self-maintenance for the normal healthy citizen. There are two lines along which the fulfillment of this duty may be sought. One would consist in providing access to the means of production, the other in guaranteeing to the individual a certain share in the common stock."[37]

All three versions of early twentieth-century English "new liberalism" are committed to the principle that the state has a duty to adopt constructive policies that make people better off, partly by creating opportunities for the less well-off, and so to a rejection of laissez-faire individualism, i.e., libertarianism.

More reason to reject the Roosevelt-changed-the-meaning-of-the-words-in-the-30s story is to be found in the facts that early twentieth-century American progressivism was understood to involve interventionist government policies and that in the first two decades of the century Americans used the words "progressive" and "liberal" interchangeably.

---

[34] Hobson, *Crisis of Liberalism*, 97.

[35] L.T. Hobhouse, *Liberalism* (London: Williams and Norgate, 1911), 35.

[36] Hobhouse, *Liberalism*, 45.

[37] Hobhouse, *Liberalism*, 49.

In 1913, legal scholar Charles Warren used the terms "progressive" and "liberal" interchangeably on the first page of an article on the Supreme Court.[38] In a 1916 speech, Raymond Robins, Chairman of the Progressive Party National Convention, said of Theodore Roosevelt, "When Colonel Roosevelt voiced this need and desire and declared himself as willing to serve in realizing a genuine progressive and liberal party, I in common with over four million voters responded to his call."[39] More evidence of the synonymy of "liberal" and "progressive" can be found in a 1923 editorial in the *New York Times*:

> In the name of "social justice" or "social welfare" or some other shibboleth, persons who call themselves "Liberals" at Washington and in the several States try to quicken instead of halting the tendency of government interference in every domain of life … . There is a "liberal-progressive-radical block" in Congress.[40]

Two years later, Franklin Roosevelt also identified "liberals" and "progressives":

> History … shows that the conservatives find it nearly always easy to control government at least two thirds of the time because they are united on the perfectly simple proposition of "doing nothing" and of "letting well enough alone." Progressives and liberals on the other hand have necessarily a constructive program, and on the details of this program they insist on dividing among themselves. I am convinced that a majority of the voters in this country are really progressives but are generally unable to control the government because of their subdivisions and unwillingness to agree as to method and machinery.[41]

And two years after this, Dewey indicated that the use of "liberal" as a party name to refer to progressives had been standard for some time,

---

[38] Charles Warren, "The Progressiveness of the United States Supreme Court," *Columbia Law Review* 13 (1913), 294.

[39] Raymond Robins, *Raymond Robins, Chairman of the Progressive National Convention, to the Progressives of the Country* (n.p., 1916), 3.

[40] "Why Liberal?" *New York Times* April 8, 1923, E6.

[41] Franklin Freidel, *Franklin D. Roosevelt: The Ordeal* (Boston: Little, Brown, 1954), 204.

writing in 1927, "In the United States the name "liberal," as a party designation, is *still* employed to designate a progressive in political matters" (emphasis added).[42]

One might wonder nevertheless why Roosevelt fastened on the word "liberal" as opposed to the word "progressive," which had recently been more common in American political discourse. James Reichley offers the following explanation:

> During the 1920s "progressive" became a somewhat tainted term for some of those who favored a degree of governmental activism, particularly among Democrats. On the one hand, it had an old-fashioned ring, was identified historically with the Republican party [of Theodore Roosevelt], and through its Social Gospel aspect was associated with militant Protestantism [including support for alcohol prohibition]. On the other, after the Progressive label was taken over by La Follette and his independent campaign for President in 1924, it came to connote a level of radicalism rejected by moderate activists like Al Smith and Franklin Roosevelt. Increasingly, therefore, liberal became the designation of choice among governmental activists, particularly Democrats, who did not believe in the desirability or inevitability of a fully collectivized economy.[43]

In 1941, Roosevelt gave a different explanation of his adoption of the "liberal" label, which is nonetheless consistent with Reichley's:

> I have always believed, and I have frequently stated, that my own party can succeed at the polls only so long as it continues to be the party of militant liberalism .... There is a vast number of independent voters who are unwilling to become affiliated with either party, but whose social and political outlook is definitely liberal, and whose votes have been cast for liberal candidates ... [and] millions of enrolled

[42] Dewey, *Public and Its Problems,* 134. Note that Dewey's statement conflicts with James Reichley's claim that "Before the 1920s the term 'liberal' in American political discourse usually represented, as it still does in Europe, opposition to all forms of collectivism." See A. James Reichley, *The Life of the Parties* (New York: Rowman and Littlefield, 2000), 209. Reichley also gives no evidence that establishes the relative frequency of these different uses in America.

[43] Reichley, *Life of the Parties,* 210.

> Republican voters—affiliated under the conservative Republican leadership for one reason or another—have nevertheless consistently voted for the type of government and candidates who appear under the liberal banner.[44]

Roosevelt hoped for a party realignment with liberal Democrats and liberal Republicans in the Democratic party and conservative Democrats and conservative Republicans in the Republican party. To this end, he worked to defeat conservative Democratic candidates in the primary elections of 1938. As he explained his goals, he "was interested in seeing to it that the Democratic party and the Republican party should not be merely Tweedledum and Tweedledee to each other."[45] He evidently believed that this realignment would benefit Democrats at the polls because more voters would then vote "for the type of government and candidates who appear under the liberal banner."

Roosevelt's use of the term "liberals" to refer to supporters of his New Deal policies reopened the debate, begun in England a half century earlier, about what liberalism "really" is. Former president Herbert Hoover and Senator Robert A. Taft both rejected the idea that the New Deal was a form of liberalism. Genuine liberalism, they maintained, was incompatible with the kind of expansion of government power brought about by Roosevelt's policies, and it was incompatible with the kind of government intrusion into the economy that these policies involved. In a 1936 article entitled "Liberalism—Real or New Deal?" Taft wrote:

> President Roosevelt would have us believe that he is the true liberal .... If the ultimate result of New Deal measures is to deprive the average man of freedom and opportunity and subject him to crushing taxation and monopoly prices, is that liberalism?[46]

He thought not. Ten years later, he wrote:

---

[44] Franklin D. Roosevelt, "Introduction," *Public Papers and Addresses of Franklin D. Roosevelt,* vol. 7, ed. Samuel Rosenmen (New York: Macmillan, 1941), xxxi.

[45] Roosevelt, "Introduction," xxxii.

[46] Robert A. Taft, "Liberalism—Real or New Deal?" *Young Republican* 1 (May 1936), 6.

> My objection to many of the self-confessed liberals of today is that they are constantly advocating measures to reduce freedom and particularly the freedom of the individual and freedom of thought. The definition I propose, therefore, is that to be a liberal a man must, first, believe in freedom and oppose measures which restrict it unless such restriction is absolutely necessary to preserve the freedom of others. Second, believe in the right of others to think differently from himself. Third, be open minded in the consideration and acceptance of new ideas as opposed to orthodox dogma and accepted practice.[47]

Taft believed that labor laws restricting freedom of contract violated the first principle of liberalism, and so that the New Dealers who supported them were not genuine liberals.

Eighteen years earlier, during his first presidential campaign, Hoover had made a related observation:

> It is a false liberalism that interprets itself into the government operation of commercial business. Every step of bureaucratizing the business of our country poisons the very roots of liberalism—that is, political equality, free speech, free assembly, free press, and equality of opportunity. It is the road not to more liberty, but to less liberty. Liberalism should be found not striving to spread bureaucracy but striving to set bounds to it. True liberalism seeks all legitimate freedom first in the confident belief that without such freedom the pursuit of all other blessings and benefits is vain. That belief is the foundation of all American progress, political as well as economic.[48]

Hoover was not a libertarian, and he rejected the Spencerian identification of liberalism with laissez-faire economic policies.[49] As a self-identified "progressive," he believed that the government must interfere

---

[47] Robert A. Taft, "What is a Liberal?" *Commercial and Financial Chronicle* 163, no. 4491 (1946), 2668.

[48] Herbert Hoover, "Campaign Address, New York City," October 22, 1928, *Hoover Archives*, 583, https://hoover.archives.gov/sites/default/files/research/ebooks/b2v1_full.pdf. Hoover's use here of the term "false liberalism" is more evidence that "liberalism" was understood in the 1920s to involve the kind of activist government that he opposed and that Roosevelt advocated in the 1930s, before Roosevelt used the term in the 1930s to refer to his New Deal policies.

[49] Herbert Hoover, "Address at Madison Square Garden in New York City," October 31, 1932, *Public Papers of the Presidents of the United States: Herbert Hoover*, 1932–1933 (Office of the Federal Register National Archives and Records Service General Administration, 1977), 677.

with the market to reduce the negative effects of concentrated wealth on political and business competition, so as to ensure what he called "equality of opportunity." But in Hoover's view, a true liberal would keep government interference with business to the bare minimum necessary to secure equality of opportunity. In his view, Roosevelt's New Deal went well beyond this.[50]

Three decades after Roosevelt was first elected president, Austrian economist Ludwig von Mises also rejected the New Deal understanding of liberalism. In the 1962 Preface to the first English edition of *Liberalism*, originally published in German in 1927, von Mises wrote:

> In the United States "liberal" means today a set of ideas and political postulates that in every regard are the opposite of all that liberalism meant to the preceding generations. The American self-styled liberal aims at government omnipotence, is a resolute foe of free enterprise, and advocates all-round planning by the authorities, i.e., socialism. These [U.S.] "liberals" [in the 1960s] are anxious to emphasize that they disapprove of the Russian dictator's policies not on account of their socialistic or communistic character but merely on account of their imperialistic tendencies. Every measure aiming at confiscating some of the assets of those who own more than the average or at restricting the rights of the owners of property is considered as liberal and progressive. Practically unlimited discretionary power is vested in government agencies the decisions of which are exempt from judicial review. The few upright citizens who dare to criticize this trend toward administrative despotism are branded as extremists, reactionaries, economic royalists, and Fascists. It is suggested that a free country ought not to tolerate political activities on the part of such "public enemies."[51]

Five years later, Hayek, another Austrian economist, offered a more temperate critique of contemporary American liberalism, writing that "what now claims this name [of 'liberalism'] in the United States is a direct descendent" of the Continental tradition of constructivist

[50] Herbert Hoover, *Addresses Upon the American Road* (New York: Charles Scribner's Sons, 1938), 132–37.

[51] Ludwig von Mises, *Liberalism: The Classical Tradition*, ed. Bettina Bien Greaves (Indianapolis, IN: Liberty Fund, 2005), xiii–xiv.

rationalism, which "became the ancestor of modern socialism."[52] In explaining his rejection of "what now claims the name of liberalism," Hayek distinguished two different traditions of liberalism, English liberalism and Continental liberalism. English liberalism was distinguished by two commitments: first, a commitment to limited constitutional government; second, a commitment to the idea that material prosperity arises spontaneously from free market exchanges provided that the government protects the rights of individuals against assault, theft, breach of contract, and fraud. This, in Hayek's view, was Adam Smith's most profound insight. Continental liberalism, in contrast, with its "constructivist rationalism," was unconcerned with limits on government power and assumed that consistent material prosperity can be ensured only by central planning. Hayek identified English liberalism with the thought of Hume, Smith, Burke, Macauley, and Lord Acton. He identified continental liberalism with the thought of Voltaire, Rousseau, and Condorcet and contended that it "ended up with the ideal of the unlimited powers of the majority."[53]

Because neither von Mises nor Hayek identifies any 1960s American liberal by name, it is not possible to tell who, exactly, they had in mind, but we should doubt the accuracy of their characterizations when we examine the views of one well-known 1960s American liberal, Hubert Humphrey, Democratic Senator from Minnesota and then Vice-President of the United States.[54]

In 1955, Humphrey wrote an article for *The American Scholar* entitled "Liberalism," in which he presents an accurate and nuanced history of

---

[52] F.A. Hayek, "The Principles of a Liberal Social Order," in *Studies in Philosophy, Politics, and Economics* (Chicago: University of Chicago Press, 1967), 160.

[53] Hayek, "Principles of a Liberal Social Order," 160.

[54] In 1977 Jimmy Carter used the phrase "self-described liberal Senators like Senator Humphrey." See Jimmy Carter, "Economic Stimulus Package Remarks and a Question-and-Answer Session on the Tax Rebate and Business Tax Credit Proposals," April 14, 1977, *The American Presidency Project*, https://www.presidency.ucsb.edu/documents/economic-stimulus-package-remarks-and-question-and-answer-session-the-tax-rebate-and. A day later Carter said: "Senator Humphrey who, as you know, has a very liberal—deservedly liberal—reputation." See Jimmy Carter, "Interview With the President Question-and-Answer Session With a Group of Publishers, Editors, and Broadcasters," April 15, 1977, *The American Presidency Project*, https://www.presidency.ucsb.edu/documents/interview-with-the-president-question-and-answer-session-with-group-publishers-editors-0.

liberalism and relates it to his own political principles.[55] According to Humphrey,

> Liberalism, as a political philosophy, is based on the assumption that freedom is essential for the full development of the human personality and that, therefore, men should be free.[56]

But human freedom and human development require different policies at different times, under different social conditions.

> Liberalism had barely begun to express itself as a formal political philosophy when it ran into the impact of industrialism. It grew out of an essentially pre-industrial, commercial environment and yet almost immediately had to cope with the economic, social and intellectual consequences of the Industrial Revolution. The rise of huge concentrations of wealth which dwarfed the individual rendered obsolete the society of small enterprisers which Adam Smith and Jefferson had in mind. The human values of liberalism were threatened by industrialism; and the political and economic non-interventionist doctrines of liberalism made it difficult for liberals to act to protect those values.[57]

For this reason, liberalism requires some government intervention into the economy, and as a consequence,

> Liberalism today stands generally committed to the qualified use of state power to achieve the values of freedom and human dignity. Like their ancestors, modern liberals recognize the concentration of power, whether in private or public hands, is the enemy of freedom.[58]

Humphrey goes on to identify liberalism with three policy commitments. First, a commitment to individual rights, specifically freedom of expression.[59] Second, "a form of 'mixed economy' which would include within it a diversification of ownership."[60] Third, "the welfare state," which, as he understands it, is organized to achieve four goals:

[55] Hubert H. Humphrey, "Liberalism," *The American Scholar* 24, no. 4 (1955): 419–33.

[56] Humphrey, "Liberalism," 419.

[57] Humphrey, "Liberalism," 424.

[58] Humphrey, "Liberalism," 429.

[59] Humphrey, "Liberalism," 429.

[60] Humphrey, "Liberalism," 429.

1. Equality of opportunity, understood to require at a minimum "the elimination of disparities brought about through racial and religious discrimination, and the universal availability of adequate educational facilities."[61]
2. Basic economic security for "those who are unable, through no fault of their own, to provide such security for themselves," including "aid to those who are disabled by reason of accident, illness, youth or old age; minimum wage legislation and unemployment insurance for all workers; and aid to economically disadvantaged groups through the support of labor unions, consumer organizations, small farmers and independent business."[62]
3. Reduction in "great disparities in the distribution of wealth" and "a closer coincidence between the income of the individual and his contribution to society."[63]
4. Full employment.[64]

Humphrey explicitly rejects direct government control of the economy to achieve these goals.

> Government power would be exercised through the indirect controls of fiscal and budgetary policy, rather than through direct physical control and central committee planning .... The liberalism of today does not seek the abolition of the price system, but it does seek the regulation and control of the profit system so as to bring about modifications to suit the requirements of a changing world ... thus invoking the agency of government to protect and assist the individual.[65]

Does Humphrey's liberalism refer to "a set of ideas and political postulates that in every regard are the opposite of all that liberalism meant to the preceding generations," as von Mises contends? No. T.H. Green, G.W.E. Russell, R.B Haldane, H.L. Samuel, J.A. Hobson, L.T. Hobhouse, and W. S. Churchill all understood liberalism in a similar way, as shown above. Are

[61] Humphrey, "Liberalism," 431.
[62] Humphrey, "Liberalism," 431.
[63] Humphrey, "Liberalism," 431.
[64] Humphrey, "Liberalism," 431.
[65] Humphrey, "Liberalism," 429.

Humphrey's ideas "a direct descendent" of the Continental tradition of constructivist rationalism as opposed to the tradition of English liberalism, as Hayek contends? No. The goals of equal opportunity, basic financial security for the needy, reduction of disparities in wealth, and full employment were all endorsed by these Englishmen in the late nineteenth- and early twentieth-centuries, and there is nothing un-English about them.

Humphrey's thought that "liberalism ... is based on the assumption that freedom is essential for the full development of the human personality and that, therefore, men should be free" also had deep roots in English liberalism. John Stuart Mill opened *On Liberty* with a passage from Wilhelm von Humboldt's *The Limits of State Action*:[66]

> The grand, leading principle, towards which every argument unfolded in these pages directly converges, is the absolute and essential importance of human development in its richest diversity.[67]

Green, Hobson and Hobhouse all followed Mill in endorsing the idea that the fundamental purpose of free institutions is human development.[68] In endorsing this idea, Humphrey thus placed himself squarely in the tradition of English liberalism.[69]

---

[66] Wilhelm von Humboldt, *The Limits of State Action*, ed. J.W. Burrow (Indianapolis, IN: Liberty Fund, 1969), 48. Humboldt wrote this treatise in the early 1780s, but it was first published in German in 1852 and first published in English in 1854.

[67] John Stuart Mill, *On Liberty*, in *Collected Works of John Stuart Mill*, vol. 18, ed. John M. Robson (Toronto: University of Toronto Press, 1977), 215.

[68] See Green, "Liberal Legislation and Freedom of Contract"; Hobson, *Crisis in Liberalism*; and Hobhouse, *Liberalism*. Dewey also embraced this Millian understanding of liberalism. See John Dewey, *Individualism, Old and New* (Lanham, MD: Prometheus Books, 1999), 15–17, 26–28, 35–49, 60–71, 80–83; and John Dewey, *Freedom and Culture* (Amherst, NY: Prometheus Books, 1989), 96–101.

[69] Hayek did once observe, though, that Mill's liberalism was not entirely faithful to the "true individualism" which he took to be the essence of "English liberalism" for the reason that it drew too many elements from continental liberalism. See F.A. Hayek, "Individualism: True and False," in *The Collected Works of F.A. Hayek*, vol. 13, ed. Bruce Caldwell (Chicago: University of Chicago Press, 2010), 20.

6

'Classical Liberalism'

Abstract This chapter investigates the history of the term "classical liberalism" and identifies some thinkers who have identified themselves, or have been identified by others, as "classical liberals." "Classical liberalism" is now generally understood to refer to the free market philosophies of F.A. Hayek, Ludwig von Mises, Milton Friedman, and James Buchanan, among others. For this reason, the term is useful, but its usefulness should not mislead us into thinking that this is what nineteenth-century Britons generally understood "liberalism" to be. The evidence presented in the previous chapters shows this to be false.

Keywords Classical liberalism · F.A. Hayek · Ludwig von Mises · Milton Friedman · James Buchanan · Libertarianism · Neoliberalism

Although their characterizations of 1960s American liberalism are inaccurate, von Mises and Hayek were quite right that what was being called "liberalism" in 1960s America was very different from what they—and Hoover and Taft—had understood liberalism to be earlier in the century, and as a result Hayek struggled to find the right label for himself. In the Postscript to *The Constitution of Liberty*, entitled "Why I Am Not a

P. de Marneffe, *The Myth of Classical Liberalism*, Palgrave Studies in Classical Liberalism,
https://doi.org/10.1007/978-3-032-14319-8_6

Conservative," Hayek writes that he had always regarded himself as a liberal, but in the U.S., this term now generates misunderstanding because of its association with a kind government management of the economy which he opposes. For this reason, he observes, some have chosen the word "libertarian" to refer to the kind of liberalism that he endorses, but he finds this term "singularly unattractive ... it carries too much the flavor of a manufactured term and of a substitute."[1] Hayek goes on to write, "The more I learn about the evolution of ideas, the more I have become aware that I am simply an unrepentant Old Whig—with the stress on 'old.'" But he sensibly recognizes that this label might not be ideal as a matter of "practical politics."[2]

The kind of liberalism that Hayek endorsed is now known as "classical liberalism." To my knowledge, he never explicitly adopted this label,[3] but he did once call his kind liberalism "classical British liberalism"[4] and others who have endorsed this form of liberalism, such as James Buchanan, have explicitly identified themselves as "classical liberals."[5] Buchanan, like Hayek and Milton Friedman a Nobel Prize-winning economist, identifies the classical liberal creed with "support for limited government, constitutional democracy, free trade, private property, rule of law, open franchise, and federalism" and he identifies Hayek as an intellectual leader of classical liberal thought.[6]

It is unclear when the term "classical liberalism" was first used to refer to this form of liberalism. According to John Maynard Keynes, "The 'classical economists' was a name invented by Marx to cover Ricardo and James Mill and their predecessors, that is to say for the founders of the

---

[1] Hayek, *Constitution of Liberty* (Chicago: University of Chicago Press, 1960) 408.

[2] Hayek, *Constitution of Liberty*, 409.

[3] James Buchanan indicates that Hayek identified himself as a "classical liberal" with these words in Hayek's Postscript to *The Constitution of Liberty*, "Why I Am Not a Conservative," but he did not. See James M. Buchanan, *Why I, Too, Am Not a Conservative: The Normative Vision of Classical Liberalism* (Northampton, MA: Elgar, 2005), 1.

[4] F.A. Hayek, "Liberalism," in *New Studies in Philosophy, Politics, Economics and the History of Ideas* (Chicago: University of Chicago Press, 1978), 128.

[5] James Buchanan, "The Soul of Classical Liberalism," *The Independent Review* 5, no. 1 (2000), 111; Buchanan, *Why I, Too, Am Not a Conservative*, 1, 9, 98.

[6] Buchanan, "Soul of Classical Liberalism," 112.

theory which culminated in the Ricardian economics."[7] Marx also used the phrase "classical political economy" in *Capital*,[8] which might have suggested to some the phrase "classical political economy liberalism" as another way of referring to what was also known as "Manchester Liberalism," and which is naturally shortened to "classical liberalism." But the *Merriam-Webster Dictionary* identifies the date of the first known use of "classical liberalism" as 1856, a decade before *Capital* was first published. *Merriam-Webster* attributes this phrase to one Virginia Anderson, but provides no citation, and consequently one cannot tell who Anderson was or where she was writing or the context in which the phrase first appeared.[9] The first place I know of where someone identified himself as a classical liberal is von Mises's *Liberalism*, first published in 1927. Although von Mises does not explicitly identify himself there as "a classical liberal," he uses the term "classical liberalism" in four different places[10] to refer to the kind of non-interventionist political and economic principles that he endorses, and which are incompatible with the interventionist New Deal liberalism that he equated with "socialism."[11]

Whatever its historical origins, the term "classical liberalism" is useful, but we should be careful not to be misled by it. The word "classical" suggests that there was a time and place in the past—in this case, eighteenth- and nineteenth-century England—when "liberalism" referred

---

[7] John Maynard Keynes, *The General Theory of Employment, Interest, and Money* (New York: Harcourt, Brace, & World, 1936), 3n1. See, for example, Karl Marx, *Capital: A Critique of Political Economy*, vol. 1, trans. Samuel Moore and Edward Aveling (Chicago: Charles H. Kerr, 1909), 385.

[8] Marx, *Capital*, 22, 68n41, 348, 351, 354.

[9] "Classical liberalism." *Merriam-Webster.com Dictionary*, Merriam-Webster, https://www.merriam-webster.com/dictionary/classical%20liberalism. Accessed 27 Oct. 2024.

[10] Ludwig von Mises, *Liberalism: The Classical Tradition*, ed. Bettina Bien Greaves (Indianapolis, IN: Liberty Fund, 2005), xiv, 68, 119, 153. The first use of the term "classical liberalism" that I know of by a historian of liberalism who was not himself a classical liberal is in Harry K. Girvetz, *From Wealth to Welfare—An Evolution of Liberalism* (Stanford: Stanford University Press, 1950), 13.

[11] Mises, *Liberalism*, xiv. In a 1937 letter to Walter Lippmann, Hayek uses the term "classical liberalism" to refer to nineteenth-century liberalism. See Angus Burgin, *The Great Persuasion: Reinventing Markets Since the Depression* (Cambridge, MA: Harvard University Press, 2012), 64.

unambiguously to what we now call "classical liberalism."[12] But the term "liberalism" was not used at all in eighteenth-century England and therefore did not refer to any political doctrine then.[13] Nor, as we have seen, did "liberalism" have a single doctrinal meaning when it came into general use in Britain in the first half of the nineteenth century. Although mid-nineteenth-century Britons who identified themselves as "liberals" did hold that government intervention into the economy should be kept to a minimum, they did not all have the same views of what the relevant minimum was. Some, like Spencer, believed that the relevant minimum was limited to the enforcement of the criminal and civil laws necessary to protect person and property. Others, like Macauley, thought the relevant minimum included laws regulating working hours for women and children. So already, in mid-nineteenth-century England, there was substantial disagreement about the proper role of the government in regulating the market, and this disagreement increased as the century progressed. For this reason, it is an error to think that there was a time—a classical period—when "liberalism" referred unambiguously to any specific doctrine about how much government intervention into the economy is warranted.

An additional observation that might be made about the term "classical liberalism" is that there were eighteenth-century thinkers other than Adam Smith who might now be anachronistically identified as "liberals" and some of them advocated a more active role for government than Smith did,[14] Johann Gottlieb Fichte, for example. Fichte was a committed republican whose *Foundations of Natural Right* was, according to a leading commentator, an "attempt to establish the basic principles of a

[12] This incorrect supposition is suggested, for example, by Milton Friedman in *Capitalism and Freedom* (Chicago: University of Chicago Press, 1962), 7–8.

[13] Pocock writes: "The term ['liberalism'] was not used in the eighteenth century, where the adjective 'liberal' did not bear its modern meaning, and though elements were present which would in due course be assembled by means of this formula, there was no system of doctrine corresponding to its later use." See J.G.A. Pocock, *The Machiavellian Moment: Florentine Political Thought and the Atlantic Republican Tradition* (Princeton, NJ: Princeton University Press, 2003), 579.

[14] Adam Smith identified only three duties of "the sovereign": national defense; protecting each member of society from interpersonal wrongs by others; and creating and maintaining certain public institutions, such as schools, and public works, such as roads, bridges and canals. Adam Smith, *An Inquiry into the Nature and Causes of the Wealth of Nations*, vol. 2, ed. Edwin Cannan (London: Methuen, 1904), 150 (Book IV, Chapter IX).

liberal political order."[15] In 1797 Fichte argued that there is a right to subsistence—which necessarily involves the redistribution of wealth—and a right to gainful employment, which the government has a duty to meet.[16] Consequently, if the identification by a twentieth-century commentator of an eighteenth-century thinker as "liberal" were sufficient to make that person's views a form of "liberalism," and if the statement of this view in the eighteenth century were sufficient to make this form of liberalism "classical," then Fichte's political philosophy would be just as much a form of "classical liberalism" as Smith's.

Searching for the right label, Hayek considered "libertarian" but rejected it on aesthetic grounds, which leaves unanswered the question of whether Hayek is properly considered a libertarian. In Chap. 3, I defined libertarianism as the view that the only legitimate function of government is to protect individuals from interpersonal wrongs, such as assault and theft.[17] Understood in this way, Hayek was not a libertarian because he believed the government has a legitimate role in regulating the money supply, preventing monopolies from forming, providing poverty relief, and funding primary and secondary education.[18] Milton Friedman, another classical liberal, held a similar position.[19] Buchanan, too,

---

[15] Frederick Neuhouser, "Introduction," in *Foundations of Natural Right*, ed. Frederick Neuhouser (New York: Cambridge University Press, 2000), vii.

[16] Fichte writes: "To be able to live is the absolute, inalienable property of all human beings . . . . A principle of all rational state constitutions is that everyone ought to be able to live from his labor . . . and the state must make arrangements to insure this . . . . [A]ll property rights are grounded in the contract of all with all, which states: "we are all entitled to keep this on the condition that we let you have what is yours." Therefore, if someone is unable to make a living from his labor, he has not been given what is absolutely his, and . . . the contract is completely cancelled with respect to him. In order to prevent property rights from being destabilized in this way, all others must (as a matter of right and in consequence of the civil contract) relinquish a portion of their own property, until he is able to live.—As soon as someone suffers from need, that portion of others' property that would be required to spare him from such need no longer belongs to those others; rather, it rightfully belongs to the one in need. The civil contract must provide for such a repartitioning of property." See J. G. Fichte, *Foundations of Natural Right*, ed. Frederick Neuhouser, trans. Michael Baur (New York: Cambridge University Press, 2000), 185–86.

[17] See Matt Zwolinski and John Tomasi, *The Individualists* (Princeton, NJ: Princeton University Press, 2023) for nuanced discussion of the different ways the term "libertarianism" can be understood.

[18] F.A. Hayek, "The Principles of a Liberal Social Order," in *Studies in Philosophy, Politics, and Economics* (Chicago: University of Chicago Press, 1967), 324–27, 265, 285–86, 377–78.

[19] Friedman, *Capitalism and Freedom*, 65, 104–6, 159, 229.

endorsed these views and held in addition that intergenerational bequests should be taxed for the sake of fairness.[20] But the term "libertarian" is also used in a broader way. The term is used to refer to members of what Matt Zwolinksi and John Tomasi have called "the Liberty Movement: that loose group of intellectuals and activists united in their support of free markets and limited government."[21] And in this broader sense, classical liberals, such as Hayek, Friedman and Buchanan, are libertarians.

Some scholars now refer to classical liberalism as "neoliberalism,"[22] but classical liberals themselves have rarely identified themselves this way. Milton Friedman, who implicitly identified himself as a classical liberal in 1962,[23] also once implicitly identified himself as a neoliberal, a decade earlier, in an essay entitled "Neo-Liberalism and Its Prospects."[24] But, as far as I can tell and for reasons unknown, he never used this term again. The terms "neoliberalism" and "neoliberal" are now more commonly used as terms of disparagement by those on the political left.[25] But whether we call the liberalism of Hayek, Friedman and Buchanan "classical liberalism" or "neoliberalism," it is important to recognize that this form of liberalism is only one of the many forms of liberalism that have been endorsed by self-identified liberals over the past two centuries.[26]

---

[20] James M. Buchanan, "Rules for a Fair Game: Contractarian Notes on Distributive Justice," in *Liberty, Market and the State* (New York: New York University Press, 1985), 133–34.

[21] Zwolinski and Tomasi, *Individualists*, 17.

[22] See, for example, Kevin Vallier, "Neoliberalism" *Stanford Encyclopedia of Philosophy*, ed. Edward N. Zalta, https://plato.stanford.edu/entries/neoliberalism/; and Samuel Moyn, *Liberalism Against Itself* (New Haven, CT: Yale University Press, 2023), 5, 85, 104, 111 (referring to the views of Hayek).

[23] Friedman, *Capitalism and Freedom*, 8.

[24] Milton Friedman, "Neo-Liberalism and Its Prospects," in *The Indispensable Milton Friedman: Essays on Politics and Economics*, ed. Lanny Ebenstein (Washington, D.C.: Regnery, 2012). Originally published in 1951.

[25] See Philip Mirowski and Dieter Plehwe, eds., *The Road from Mount Pelerin: The Making of the Neoliberal Thought Collective* (Cambridge, MA: Harvard University Press, 2009), xvi, 7–8; and Cass R. Sunstein, *Liberalism: In Defense of Freedom* (Cambridge, MA: MIT Press, 2025), 14.

[26] As Amanda Anderson puts it, "neoliberalism is entirely distinct from, and incompatible with, the long traditions of political liberalism and social democracy that challenged narrow forms of classical economic liberalism of the sort associated with John Locke and Adam Smith." See Amanda Anderson, *Bleak Liberalism* (Chicago: Chicago University Press, 2016), 39.

7

Conclusion

Abstract This chapter briefly examines the history of the word "liberal" in America since the New Deal. Roosevelt characterized his supporters as "liberals" in the belief that this would increase public support for his policies, but in the decades that followed, successful Democratic politicians avoided the "liberal" label. This chapter offers some speculations about why.

Keywords John F. Kennedy · Lyndon Johson · Great Society · Liberals · Conservatives · The left · The right

I opened this book with three questions and sketched the answers provided by what has become the myth of classical liberalism. According to this story, "liberalism" originally referred unambiguously to a doctrine of limited government and laissez-faire economic principles; Spencer, Dicey, Smith, Hoover, Taft, and Hayek all used the word properly in its original sense; Dworkin and Rawls used the word in a corrupted sense created by Roosevelt during the New Deal. This story is inaccurate. The English word "liberalism" never referred unambiguously to libertarianism. Originally, it meant a commitment to constitutionalism or republicanism.

P. de Marneffe, *The Myth of Classical Liberalism*, Palgrave Studies in Classical Liberalism,
https://doi.org/10.1007/978-3-032-14319-8_7

Then it came to mean a commitment to increasing the "power of the people." Then it came to mean different things to different authors. The sense in which Roosevelt used the word in the 1930s was already well-established in Britain in the 1880s and already well-established in America in the 1920s. So, Roosevelt did not change the meaning of the word; he simply used an ambiguous word in one of its established uses.

Why did Goldwater identify himself in 1960 as "a conservative" and not as "a liberal," even though his recent political forbears had identified themselves as liberals? Because in 1960 "liberals" were understood to be supporters of the New Deal and Goldwater opposed the growth of federal government that the New Deal involved. How could Hayek and Dworkin have meant such different things by "liberalism" in 1978? Hayek identified liberalism with principles warranting the kind of view that Hoover and Taft endorsed; Dworkin identified it with principles warranting the kind of view that Humphrey endorsed. Why did it make sense for Spencer to claim in 1884 that only libertarianism is "true liberalism"? Because he understood liberalism as a principled commitment to equality before the law and an end to all legally established economic privileges, and he saw libertarianism as the only principled basis for these liberal positions. Why did it make sense for Rawls to claim in 1996 that libertarianism is "not liberalism at all"? Because he understood liberalism to be essentially committed to ensuring "all citizens . . . the all-purpose means necessary for them to take intelligent and effective advantage of their basic freedoms," and he did not believe that libertarianism ensures this.[1] Neither Hayek nor Dworkin, Spencer nor Rawls was misusing the term. They were all using it in accordance with an established meaning. For this reason, there is no basis in history for claiming that any one of these views is "true liberalism" and that the other versions are false.

In the late 1930s, Roosevelt sought to bring about a party realignment, with liberal Democrats and Republicans in the Democratic Party and conservative Democrats and Republicans in the Republican Party. He thought this would benefit Democrats at the polls because more

[1] John Rawls, *Political Liberalism*, paperback ed. (New York: Columbia University Press, 1996), lviii-lix.

voters would then vote "for the type of government and candidates who appear under the liberal banner."[2] Things did not turn out this way. Two decades later, Democratic candidates for national office no longer regarded the liberal label as an electoral advantage.

The Democratic presidential nominee in 1960 was John F. Kennedy and I have found only one place where Kennedy explicitly identified himself as "a liberal"—when accepting the nomination of the New York Liberal Party. On that occasion, he said:

> What do our opponents mean when they apply to us the label "Liberal?" If by "Liberal" they mean, as they want people to believe, someone who is soft in his policies abroad, who is against local government, and who is unconcerned with the taxpayer's dollar, then the record of this party and its members demonstrate that we are not that kind of "Liberal." But if by a "Liberal" they mean someone who looks ahead and not behind, someone who welcomes new ideas without rigid reactions, someone who cares about the welfare of the people—their health, their housing, their schools, their jobs, their civil rights, and their civil liberties—someone who believes we can break through the stalemate and suspicions that grip us in our policies abroad, if that is what they mean by a "Liberal," then I'm proud to say I'm a "Liberal."[3]

Kennedy goes on to characterize his liberalism with an abstract philosophical statement that even Herbert Hoover might have endorsed:

> I believe in human dignity as the source of national purpose, in human liberty as the source of national action, in the human heart as the source of national compassion, and in the human mind as the source of our invention and our ideas. It is, I believe, the faith in our fellow citizens as individuals and as people that lies at the heart of the liberal faith. For liberalism is not so much a party creed or set of fixed

[2] Franklin D. Roosevelt, "Introduction," *Public Papers and Addresses of Franklin D. Roosevelt*, vol. 7, ed. Samuel Rosenmen (New York: Macmillan, 1941), xxxi.

[3] John F. Kennedy, "Speech of Senator John F. Kennedy, Commodore Hotel, New York, NY, Acceptance of Party Nomination," September 14, 1960, *The American Presidency Project*, https://www.presidency.ucsb.edu/documents/speech-senator-john-f-kennedy-commodore-hotel-new-york-ny-acceptance-party-nomination.

> platform promises as it is an attitude of mind and heart, a faith in man's ability through the experiences of his reason and judgment to increase for himself and his fellow men the amount of justice and freedom and brotherhood which all human life deserves.[4]

I have been unable to identify any other instance when Kennedy publicly identified himself as "a liberal" in 1960 or any other year.

Four years later, in 1964, the Democratic presidential nominee was Lyndon Johnson. Asked in an interview whether he identified himself as a "liberal" or a "conservative," Johnson deflected the question.

> Well, I don't believe in labels. I want to do the best I can, all the time. I want to be progressive without getting both feet off the ground at the same time. I want to be prudent without having my mind closed to anything that is new or different. I have often said that I was proud that I was a free man first and an American second, and a public servant third and a Democrat fourth, in that order, and I guess as a Democrat, if I had to take—place a label on myself, I would want to be a progressive who is prudent.[5]

Once elected president, Johnson occasionally identified himself as "a liberal,"[6] but I have found only two instances, and in both cases he was addressing a group of Democrats whom, he could assume, would have identified themselves the same way.[7] In 1968, the Democratic presidential nominee was Hubert Humphrey and although he had for years

---

[4] Kennedy, "Acceptance of Party Nomination."

[5] Lyndon B. Johnson, "Transcript of Television and Radio Interview Conducted by Representatives of Major Broadcast Services," March 15, 1964, *The American Presidency Project*, https://www.presidency.ucsb.edu/documents/transcript-television-and-radio-interview-conducted-representatives-major-broadcast.

[6] The claim of Ellis and Stimson is therefore incorrect that "John Kennedy would not be the last liberal president. But he would be the last who would call himself a liberal." See Christopher Ellis and James A. Stimson, "Symbolic Ideology in the American Electorate," *Electoral Studies* 28, no. 3 (2009), 397.

[7] Lyndon B. Johnson, "Remarks at the Democratic Congressional Dinner in the D.C. Armory," June 24, 1965, *The American Presidency Project*, https://www.presidency.ucsb.edu/documents/remarks-the-democratic-congressional-dinner-the-dc-armory; Lyndon B. Johnson, "Remarks in Atlantic City at the International Ladies' Garment Workers Union Convention," May 25, 1968, *The American Presidency Project*, https://www.presidency.ucsb.edu/documents/remarks-atlantic-city-the-international-ladies-garment-workers-union-convention.

identified himself as a liberal,[8] he did not place this political identity at the center of his presidential campaign.

Why did leading Democrats in the 1960s avoid the "liberal" label when Roosevelt had made so much of it in the 1930s? Ellis and Stimson write that "Between 1963, when the Kennedy assassination made Lyndon Johnson president, and 1967, the third year of LBJ's Great Society, the ranks of self-identified liberals fell by 10.5 points—about one fourth—and never recovered."[9] In 1936, roughly 35% of voters identified as "liberal" and roughly 35% identified as "conservative." In 1967, only 20% identified themselves as "liberal" and 30% identified themselves as "conservative." This trend continued for the rest of the century.[10]

Ellis and Stimson identify four factors that might explain why the number of self-identified liberals decreased in the 1960s:

1. The focus of Roosevelt's New Deal was on improving the condition of the common man, the ordinary working man; the focus of Johnson's Great Society was "to bring benefits and political voice to an underclass of Americans who lived below the common standard," many of whom did not work.[11]
2. Poverty programs directed a great deal of federal money to the urban poor and "set up governance over that spending by boards that largely excluded public officials and called for 'maximum feasible participation' of the poor."[12] As a consequence, politically and administratively inexperienced persons were managing large amounts of federal taxpayer dollars.

---

[8] See Hubert H. Humphrey, "Liberalism," *The American Scholar* 24, no. 4 (1955): 419–33.

[9] Ellis and Stimson, "Symbolic Ideology," 397.

[10] Roper Center for Public Opinion Research, Prevention Magazine, The Tokyo Broadcasting System, et al., "Political Ideology, Three-Way, 'Describe Your Views' (1976–2014)" (Roper Center for Public Opinion Research, 2024), https://ropercenter.cornell.edu/ipoll/trend/5040ff44-3006-4322-acd8-01bbe3754efc.

[11] Ellis and Stimson, "Symbolic Ideology," 398.

[12] Ellis and Stimson, "Symbolic Ideology," 398.

3. The common working man benefited by the New Deal was perceived to be white; the beneficiaries of Johnson's Great Society programs were perceived to be predominantly Black.[13]
4. Despite the increased availability of federal funds to urban Black communities, there were race riots in these communities in the summers of 1965 and 1966.

Another possible factor is the unprecedented increase in violent crime in the 1960s and 70s. Because "liberals" were associated with "soft on crime" policies, such as procedural safeguards for criminal defendants, this, too, might have led some voters not to identify themselves as "liberal."

Whatever the explanation, the "liberal" label was also avoided by Jimmy Carter, the only successful Democratic presidential candidate between Lyndon Johnson and Bill Clinton. When asked whether he was liberal or conservative, Carter answered that he was liberal in some ways, conservative in others, and moderate in others. He didn't vote for or against a policy on the basis of ideology; he voted for or against it on its merits.[14] Michael Dukakis, the Democratic presidential nominee in 1988, took the same tack. On Nightline with Ted Koppel, he said, "All of us have a combination of liberal and conservative about us."[15] No doubt trying to be helpful, a well-known Dukakis ally publicly defended him against the "liberal" label a month earlier. As reported in the *New York Times*:

> Former House Speaker Thomas P. O'Neill, Jr., an unabashed liberal, today rebutted Republican charges that Michael S. Dukakis is so liberal he is "out of the mainstream" of American politics. "I'm an old-fashioned liberal," Mr. O'Neill said, contrasting himself and

[13] Ellis and Stimson, "Symbolic Ideology," 398.

[14] Jimmy Carter, "Economic Stimulus Package Remarks and a Question-and-Answer Session on the Tax Rebate and Business Tax Credit Proposals, April 14, 1977. *The American Presidency Project*, https://www.presidency.ucsb.edu/documents/economic-stimulus-package-remarks-and-question-and-answer-session-the-tax-rebate-and.

[15] Ted Koppel, host, *Nightline*, October 25, 1988, https://www.youtube.com/watch?v=Mrh-Tz8xMMc, at 9:35.

> Governor Dukakis, a fellow Massachusettsan. "He's a progressive, he's a technician, he's a leader."[16]

O'Neill was happy enough to identify himself as "an old-fashioned liberal," but he was no longer running for office.

Today news and polling organizations use the term "liberal" generically to mean "left of center" and "conservative" to mean "right of center," "very liberal" to mean "well left of center" and "very conservative" to mean "well right of center." How did "liberals" come to have this generic left of center meaning? According to Hyrum Lewis and Verlan Lewis, American journalists started using the terms "left" and "right" to refer to different American ideological orientations only in the 1920s.[17] Then in the 1930s, when the term "liberals" was increasingly associated with supporters of Roosevelt's New Deal policies and "conservatives" was increasingly associated with those who opposed these policies, journalists increasingly identified "liberals" with "the left" and "conservatives" with "the right."[18] "Liberals" and those "on the left" were initially understood to be those who supported the New Deal and "conservatives" and those "on the right" were understood to be those who opposed it,[19] but, as the Democratic Party was increasingly identified with other policy goals, such as racial equality, sex equality, an end to the Vietnam War, and environmental protection, these other goals, too, came to be seen as "liberal" and "on the left," though they were quite different from the goals that distinguished "liberals" and "conservatives" in the 1930s.

Reflecting on the history of the English words "liberals" and "liberalism," it is easy to regret the debased generic use of these words by journalists, pollsters, and pundits. This is because, in some historical sense, most Americans are liberals. We are republicans, not monarchists. We believe in government of the people, by the people, and for the people. We believe that the exercise of official power is properly limited

[16] "O'Neill, Avowed Liberal, Contrasts Dukakis," *New York Times*, September 27, 1988.

[17] Hyrum Lewis and Verlan Lewis, *The Myth of Left and Right* (New York: Oxford University Press, 2023), 21.

[18] Lewis and Lewis, *Myth of Left and Right*, 22.

[19] Lewis and Lewis, *Myth of Left and Right*, 24–25.

by laws, by a constitution. And these things are worthy of allegiance. We are also grateful for the changes brought about by social reformers in the past—universal suffrage, universal education, retirement security, worker health and safety regulations, and civil rights laws—all policies advocated at the time by self-identified liberals. Reading Kennedy's generous words above, we might wish, too, that we could recognize a shared political faith, one that, given the history of the word, might fairly be called "liberalism." We might wish for a common understanding of liberalism that is something more than the policies that self-identified "conservatives" currently hate. This is not likely to happen any time soon, but, looking back, we can still appreciate what self-identified liberals once accomplished and recognize that most of what is good in American political society comes from what was once known as "liberalism."

Bibliography

Anderson, Amanda. *Bleak Liberalism*. Chicago: University of Chicago Press, 2016.

Arblaster, Anthony. *The Rise and Decline of Western Liberalism*. Oxford: Basil Blackwell, 1984.

Arbuthnot, Harriet, *The Journal of Mrs. Arbuthnot 1820–32*, in two volumes. Edited by Francis Bamford and the Duke of Wellington. London: Macmillan, 1950.

Barry, Brian. *Why Social Justice Matters*. New York: Polity Press, 2005.

Beer, Samuel H. "Liberalism and the National Idea." In *Left, Right, and Center: Essays on Liberalism and Conservativism in the United States*. Edited by Robert A. Goldwin. Chicago: Rand McNally, 1965.

Bell, Duncan. "What is Liberalism?" *Political Theory*, 42, no. 6 (2014): 682–715.

Blease, W. Lyon. *A Short History of English Liberalism*. London: T. Fisher Unwin, 1913.

Brady, Alexander. *William Huskisson and Liberal Reform*, 2nd edition. London: Frank Cass, 1967.

Brock, W.R. *Lord Liverpool and Liberal Toryism, 1820 to 1827*. London: Frank Cass, 1967.

Brougham, Henry. "State of Parties." *Edinburgh Review* 46 (1827): 415–432.

P. de Marneffe, *The Myth of Classical Liberalism*, Palgrave Studies in Classical Liberalism,
https://doi.org/10.1007/978-3-032-14319-8

Brown, David. "The Press." In *The Oxford Handbook of Modern British Political History, 1800-2000*, edited by David Brown, Robert Crowcraft, and Gordon Pentland. New York: Oxford University Press, 2018.

Buchanan, James M. "Rules for a Fair Game: Contractarian Notes on Distributive Justice." *In Liberty, Market and the State.* New York: New York University Press, 1985.

Buchanan, James M. "The Soul of Classical Liberalism." *The Independent Review* 5, no. 1 (2000): 111–119.

Buchanan, James M. *Why I, Too, Am Not a Conservative: The Normative Vision of Classical Liberalism.* Northampton, MA: Elgar, 2005.

Buckingham, J.S. *The Parliamentary Review.* London: Simpkin and Marshall, 1833.

Bullock, Alan, and Maurice Shock. *The Liberal Tradition from Fox to Keynes.* New York: New York University Press, 1957.

Burgin, Angus. *The Great Persuasion: Reinventing Markets Since the Depression.* Cambridge, MA: Harvard University Press, 2012.

Canning, George. "Negotiations Relative to Spain." *House of Commons Debate,* 30 April 1823. Vol. 8 of *Hansard 1803–2005,* col. 1483. https://api.parliament.uk/historic-hansard/commons/1823/apr/30/negotiations-relative-to-spain#S2V0008P0_18230430_HOC_42.

Cappon, Lester J. *The Adams-Jefferson Letters.* Chapel Hill, NC: University of North Carolina Press, 1959.

Carter, Jimmy. "Economic Stimulus Package Remarks and a Question-and-Answer Session on the Tax Rebate and Business Tax Credit Proposals. April 14, 1977. *The American Presidency Project.* https://www.presidency.ucsb.edu/documents/economic-stimulus-package-remarks-and-question-and-answer-session-the-tax-rebate-and.

Carter, Jimmy. "Interview With the President Question-and-Answer Session With a Group of Publishers, Editors, and Broadcasters." April 15, 1977. *The American Presidency Project.* https://www.presidency.ucsb.edu/documents/interview-with-the-president-question-and-answer-session-with-group-publishers-editors-0.

Castlereagh, Robert Stewart. *Memoirs and Correspondence of Viscount Castlereagh.* Edited by Charles Vane. London: H. Colburn, 1853.

Churchill, Winston S. *Liberalism and the Social Problem.* New York: Hodder and Stoughton, 1909.

Clark, J.C.D. *English Society 1660–1832: Religion, ideology and politics during the ancien regime.* New York: Cambridge University Press, 2000.

Clarke, Peter. *Liberals & Social Democrats*. New York: Cambridge University Press, 1978.

Cohen, Nancy. *The Reconstruction of American Liberalism, 1865–1914*. Chapel Hill: University of North Carolina Press, 2002.

Collini, Stefan. *Liberalism and Sociology: L.T. Hobhouse and Political Argument in England, 1880–1914*. New York: Cambridge University Press, 1979.

Coohill, Joseph: *Ideas of the Liberal Party: Perceptions, Agendas and Liberal Politics in the House of Commons, 1832–1852*. Oxford: Wiley-Blackwell, 2011.

Craig, David Marcellus. "Tories and the Language of 'Liberalism' in the 1820s." *English Historical Review* 135, no. 576 (2020): 1195–1228.

Croker, John Wilson. "Mr. Peel to Mr. Croker, 23 March 1820." In *The Correspondence and Diaries of the Late Right Honorable John Wilson Croker*. 2nd ed. Vol. 1. Edited and revised by Louis J. Jennings. New York: AMS Press, 1972.

Dewey, John. *The Public and Its Problems*. New York: Henry Holt and Company, 1927.

Dewey, John. *Individualism, Old and New*. Lanham, MD: Prometheus Books, 1999. Originally published in 1930.

Dewey, John. *Liberalism and Social Action*. Lanham, MD: Prometheus Books, 2000. Originally published in 1935.

Dewey, John. *Freedom and Culture*. Amherst, NY: Prometheus Books, 1989. Originally published in 1939.

Diario de Sesiones de las Cortes Generales y Extraordinarias, 1810–1813, https://app.congreso.es/est_sesiones/.

Dicey, Edward. "The Plea of a Malcontent Liberal." *Fortnightly Review* 44 (1885): 463–477.

Dworkin, Ronald. "Liberalism." In *Public and Private Morality*, edited by Stuart Hampshire. New York: Cambridge University Press, 1978.

Eccleshall, Robert. *British Liberalism: Liberal Thought from the 1640s to 1980s*. New York: Longman, 1986.

Ellis, Christopher, and James. A Stimson. "Symbolic Ideology in the American Electorate." *Electoral Studies* 28, no. 3 (2009): 388–402.

Esdaile, Charles J. *Spain in the Liberal Age*. Oxford: Blackwell, 2000.

Fawcett, Edmund. *Liberalism: The Life of an Idea*, 2nd ed. Princeton, NJ: Princeton University Press, 2018.

Fichte, J. G. *Foundations of Natural Right*. Edited by Frederick Neuhouser, translated by Michael Baur. New York: Cambridge University Press, 2000.

Freeden, Michael. *The New Liberalism: Ideology and Social Reform*. New York: Oxford University Press, 1978.

Freeden, Michael. *Liberalism: A Very Short Introduction*. New York: Oxford University Press, 2015.

Freeman, Samuel. "Illiberal Libertarians: Why Libertarianism Is Not a Liberal View." *Philosophy & Public Affairs* 30, no. 2 (2001): 105–151.

Freeman, Samuel. "Capitalism in the Classical and High Liberal Traditions." *Social Philosophy and Policy* 28, no. 2 (2011): 19–55.

Freidel, Franklin. *Franklin D. Roosevelt: The Ordeal*. Boston: Little, Brown, 1954.

Friedman, Milton. *Capitalism and Freedom*. Chicago: University of Chicago Press, 1962.

Friedman, Milton. "Neo-Liberalism and Its Prospects." In *The Indispensable Milton Friedman: Essays on Politics and Economics*. Edited by Lanny Ebenstein. Washington, D.C.: Regnery, 2012. Originally published in 1951.

Gash, Norman. *Reaction and Reconstruction in English Politics, 1832–1852*. Oxford: Oxford University Press, 1965.

Gash, Norman. *Sir Robert Peel: The Life of Sir Robert Peel after 1830*. London: Longman, 1972.

Gaus, Gerald. *The Modern Liberal Theory of Man*. London: Routledge, 1983.

Girvetz, Harry K. *From Wealth to Welfare—An Evolution of Liberalism*. Stanford: Stanford University Press, 1950.

Geuss, Raymond. *History and Illusion in Politics*. New York: Cambridge University Press, 2001.

Goldwater, Barry. *The Conscience of a Conservative*. Shepherdsville, KY: Victor Publishing, 1960.

Goodfellow, Gabriel, *The Book of Liberals: A Book for Liberals and Anti-Liberals; Being a Looking-Glass for the Former, and an Eye-Glass (or Spy-Glass) for the Latter*. Privately published, London, 1849. https://books.google.com/books?id=vKpXAAAAcAAJ&printsec=frontcover&source=gbs_ge_summary_r&cad=0#v=onepage&q&f=false, last accessed 10/5/25.

Gray, John. *Liberalism*, 2nd ed. Minneapolis, MN: University of Minnesota Press, 1995.

Green, Thomas Hill. "Lecture on Liberal Legislation and Freedom of Contract." In *Works of Thomas Hill Green. Vol. III. Miscellanies and Memoir. With a Portrait*. Edited by R.L. Nettleship. London: Longmans, Green, 1888. Originally published in 1881.

Haldane, R.B. "The Liberal Creed." *The Contemporary Review* 54 (October 1888): 461–474.
Haldane, R.B. "The New Liberalism." *The Progressive Review* 1, no. 2 (1896): 133–143.
Halevy, Elie. *The Liberal Awakening, 1815–1830*. Translated by E.I. Watkin. New York: Peter Smith, 1949.
Hallam, Henry. *The Constitutional History of England from the Accession of Henry VII to the Death of George II*. Vol. 3. Paris: L. Baudry, 1827.
Hallowell, John H. *The Decline of Liberalism as an Ideology, with Particular Reference to German Politico-Legal Thought*. Berkeley, CA: University of California Press, 1943.
Hartz, Louis. *The Liberal Tradition in America*. New York: Harcourt, Brace, 1955.
Haury, David. *The Origins of the Liberal Party and Liberal Imperialism: The Career of Charles Buller 1806–1848*. New York: Garland Publishing, 1987.
Hay, Daisy. "Liberals, *Liberales*, and *The Liberal*: A Reassessment." *European Romantic Review* 19 (2008): 307–320.
Hayek, F.A. *The Constitution of Liberty*. Chicago: University of Chicago Press, 1960.
Hayek, F.A. "The Principles of a Liberal Social Order." In *Studies in Philosophy, Politics, and Economics*. Chicago: University of Chicago Press, 1967.
Hayek, F.A. "Liberalism." In *New Studies in Philosophy, Politics, Economics and the History of Ideas*. Chicago: University of Chicago Press, 1978.
Hayek, F.A. "Individualism: True and False." In *The Collected Works of F.A. Hayek*. Vol. 13. Edited by Bruce Caldwell. Chicago: University of Chicago Press, 2010. Given as a lecture in 1945.
Hinde, Wendy. *George Canning*. London: Collins, 1973.
Hobhouse, Sir Benjamin. "Negotiations Relative to Spain." House of Commons Debate, 28 April 1823. Vol. 8 of Hansard 1803–2005, col. 1345. https://api.parliament.uk/historic-hansard/commons/1823/apr/28/negotiations-relative-to-spain.
Hobhouse, L. T. *Liberalism*. London: Williams and Norgate, 1911.
Hobson, J.A. *The Crisis of Liberalism, New Issues of Democracy*. London: P.S. King, 1909.
Hoover, Herbert. "Campaign Address, New York City." October 22, 1928. *Hoover Archives*. https://hoover.archives.gov/sites/default/files/research/ebooks/b2v1_full.pdf.

Hoover, Herbert. "Address at Madison Square Garden in New York City." October 31, 1932. *Public Papers of the Presidents of the United States: Herbert Hoover, 1932-1933*. Office of the Federal Register National Archives and Records Service General Administration, 1977.

Hoover, Herbert. "True Liberalism." In *Addresses Upon the American Road*. New York: Charles Scribner's Sons, 1938.

Humboldt, Wilhelm von. *The Limits of State Action*. Edited by J.W. Burrow. Indianapolis, IN: Liberty Fund, 1969. Originally published in 1854.

Humphrey, Hubert H. "Liberalism." *The American Scholar* 24, no. 4 (1955): 419–433.

Irwin, Douglas A. *Clashing Over Commerce*. Chicago: Chicago University Press, 2017.

Isabella, Maurizio. *Risorgimento in Exile: Italian Émigrés and the Liberal International in the Post-Napoleonic Era*. New York: Oxford University Press, 2009.

Jenkins, T.A. *The Liberal Ascendency, 1830–1886*. Basingstroke: Macmillan, 1994.

Johnson, Lyndon B. "Transcript of Television and Radio Interview Conducted by Representatives of Major Broadcast Services." March 15, 1964. *The American Presidency Project*. https://www.presidency.ucsb.edu/documents/transcript-television-and-radio-interview-conducted-representatives-major-broadcast.

Johnson, Lyndon B. "Remarks at the Democratic Congressional Dinner in the D.C. Armory." June 24, 1965. *The American Presidency Project*. https://www.presidency.ucsb.edu/documents/remarks-the-democratic-congressional-dinner-the-dc-armory.

Johnson, Lyndon B. "Remarks in Atlantic City at the International Ladies' Garment Workers Union Convention." May 25, 1968. *The American Presidency Project*. https://www.presidency.ucsb.edu/documents/remarks-atlantic-city-the-international-ladies-garment-workers-union-convention.

Johnston, Alexander. "Liberal Republican Party." In *Cyclopedia of Political Science, Political Economy, and of the Political History of the United States*. Vol. 2. Edited by John Joseph Lalor. New York: Maynard, Merrill, 1889.

Kennedy, John F. "Speech of Senator John F. Kennedy, Commodore Hotel, New York, NY, Acceptance of Party Nomination." September 14, 1960. *The American Presidency Project*. https://www.presidency.ucsb.edu/documents/speech-senator-john-f-kennedy-commodore-hotel-new-york-ny-acceptance-party-nomination.

Keynes, John Maynard. *The General Theory of Employment, Interest, and Money*. New York: Harcourt, Brace, & World, 1936.

Kinder, Donald, and Nathan Kalmoe. *Neither Liberal Nor Conservative: Ideological Innocence in the American Public*. Chicago: University of Chicago Press, 2017.

Klein, Daniel. "'Liberal' as a Political Adjective (in English), 1869–1824." *Journal of Contextual Economics—Schmollers Jahrbuch* 143 (2024): 239–261. https://doi.org/10.3790/schm.2024.380533.

Koppel, Ted, host. *Nightline*, October 25, 1988, https://www.youtube.com/watch?v=Mrh-Tz8xMMc.

Laski, Harold J. *The Rise of European Liberalism*. London: Unwin, 1962.

Leonhard, Jorn. "'*An odious but intelligible phrase*' ... Liberal im politischen Diskurs Deutschlands und Englands bis 1820–1832." *Jarhbuch zur Liberalismus-Forschung* (1996): 11–41.

Leonhard, Jorn. "From European Liberalism to the Languages of Liberalisms: The Semantics of 'Liberalism' in European Comparison." *Redescriptions: Yearbook of Political Thought and Conceptual History* 8 (2004): 17–51.

Leonhard, Jorn. "Conceptual History: The Comparative Dimension." In *Conceptual History in European Space*. Edited by Willibald Steinmetz, Michael Freeden, and Javier Fernandez-Sebastian. New York: Berghan, 2017.

Lewis, C.G. Review of "Letter from Sir Robert Peel to the Electors for the Borough of Tamworth." *Edinburgh Review* 87 (1848): 138–169.

Lewis, Hyrum, and Verlan Lewis. *The Myth of Left and* Right. New York: Oxford University Press, 2023.

Lewis, Verlan. *Ideas of Power*. New York: Cambridge University Press, 2019.

"On Liberality. '*The Liberal; Verse and Prose from the South.*' Postscript to Lord Byron." *The Council of Ten* 2 (1822): 149–158,174.

Lipset, Seymour Martin. "Americans Sneer at the Liberalism. Why?" *New York Times*, October 28, 1988.

Losurdo, Domenico. *Liberalism: A Counter-History*. Translated by Gregory Elliot. London: Verso, 2011.

Macauley, Thomas Babington. "The Ten Hours Bill (May 22, 1846)." In *The Complete Works of Thomas Babington Macauley: Speeches and Legal Studies*. New York: Sully and Kleinteich, 1900.

Macauley, Thomas Babington. "Exclusion of Judges from the House of Commons (June 1, 1853)." In *The Complete Works of Thomas Babington Macauley: Speeches and Legal Studies*. New York: Sully and Kleinteich, 1900.

Mandler, Peter. *Aristocratic Government in the Age of Reform, Whigs and Liberals, 1830–1852*. New York: Oxford University Press, 1990.

Marx, Karl. *Capital: A Critique of Political Economy*. Vol. 1. Translated by Samuel Moore and Edward Aveling. Chicago: Charles H. Kerr, 1909. Originally published in English in 1887.

McCallum, Robert B. *The Liberal Party from Earl Grey to Asquith*. London: Victor Gollancz, 1961.

McCloskey, Deirdre. *Why Liberalism Works: How True Liberal Values Produce a Freer, More Equal, More Prosperous World for All*. New Haven, CT: Yale University Press, 2019.

Milkis, Sidney M. *The President and the Parties*. New York: Oxford University Press, 1993.

Mill, John Stuart. *Principles of Political Economy, with Some of Their Applications to Social Philosophy*. Vol. 2. Boston: Charles C. Little and James Brown, 1848.

Mill, John Stuart. "Walsh's Contemporary History (1836)." In *The Collected Works of John Stuart Mill*. Vol. 6. Edited by John M. Robson. Toronto: University of Toronto Press, 1982.

Mill, John Stuart. "To John Sterling 20 October 1831." In *The Collected Works of John Stuart Mill*. Vol. 12. Edited by Francis E. Mineka. Toronto: University of Toronto Press, 1963.

Mill, John Stuart. "To John Plummer 3 October 1863." In *The Collected Works of John Stuart Mill*. Vol. 15. Edited by Francis E. Mineka. Toronto: University of Toronto Press, 1972.

Mill, John Stuart. "To Edward P. Bouverie 19 October 1868." In *The Collected Works of John Stuart Mill*. Vol. 16. Edited by Francis E. Mineka and Dwight N. Lindley. Toronto: University of Toronto Press, 1972.

Mill, John Stuart. *On Liberty*. In *The Collected Works of John Stuart Mill*. Vol. 18. Edited by John M. Robson. Toronto: University of Toronto Press, 1977. Originally published in 1859.

Mill, John Stuart. "Thoughts on Parliamentary Reform." In *The Collected Works of John Stuart Mill*. Vol. 19. Edited by John M. Robson. Toronto: University of Toronto Press, 1977. Originally published in 1859.

Mill, John Stuart. "The Westminster Election of 1865." In *The Collected Works of John Stuart Mill*. Vol. 28. Edited by John M. Robson and Bruce L. Kinzer. Toronto: University of Toronto Press, 1988.

Mill, John Stuart. "W.E. Gladstone, 21 July 1866." In *The Collected Works of John Stuart Mill.* Vol. 28. Edited by John M. Robson and Bruce L. Kinzer. Toronto: University of Toronto Press, 1988.

Mirowski, Philip, and Dieter Plehwe, eds. *The Road from Mount Pelerin: The Making of the Neoliberal Thought Collective.* Cambridge, MA: Harvard University Press, 2009.

Mises, Ludwig von. *Liberalism: The Classical Tradition.* Edited by Bettina Bien Greaves. Indianapolis, IN: Liberty Fund, 2005. Originally published in German in 1927.

Morley, John. *The Life of Richard Cobden.* London: T. Fisher Unwin, 1903.

Moyn, Samuel. *Liberalism Against Itself.* New Haven, CT: Yale University Press, 2023.

Murray, James A. H. *A New English Dictionary on Historical Principles.* Vol 6. Oxford: Clarendon Press, 1928.

Nefftzer, Auguste. "Liberalism." In *Cyclopedia of Political Science, Political Economy, and of the Political History of the United States.* Vol. 2. Edited by John Joseph Lalor. New York: Maynard, Merrill, 1889.

Neill, Thomas P. *The Rise and Decline of Liberalism.* Milwaukee, WI: Bruce Publishing, 1953.

Neuhouser, Frederick. "Introduction." In *Foundations of Natural Right.* Edited by Frederick Neuhouser, translated by Michael Baur. New York: Cambridge University Press, 2000.

Nozick, Robert. *Anarchy, State, and Utopia.* New York: Basic Books, 1974.

"O'Neill, Avowed Liberal, Contrasts Dukakis." *New York Times*, September 27, 1988.

Palmer, R.R., Joel Colton, and Lloyd Kramer. *History of the Modern World: Since* 1815. New York: McGraw Hill, 2007.

Parry, Jonathan. *The Rise and Fall of Liberal Government in Victorian Britain.* New Haven, CT: Yale University Press, 1993.

Peel, Robert. "Address to the Electors of Tamworth." *The Times* (London), 18 December 1834.

Pocock, J.G.A. *The Machiavellian Moment: Florentine Political Thought and the Atlantic Republican Tradition.* Princeton, NJ: Princeton University Press, 2003.

Prest, John. *Lord John Russell.* London: Macmillan, 1972.

R.S. "The Candid. No. I." *Blackwood's Edinburgh Magazine* 12 (1823): 108–124.

Rawls, John. *Political Liberalism*. Paperback edition. New York: Columbia University Press, 1996.

Reichley, A. James. *The Life of the Parties*. New York: Rowman and Littlefield, 2000.

Reid, Andrew. *Why I Am a Liberal, Being the Personal Confessions of Faith by the Best Minds of the Liberal Party*. London: Cassell, 1885.

Robins, Raymond. *Raymond Robins, Chairman of the Progressive National Convention, to the Progressives of the Country*. n.p., 1916.

Robinson, David. "The Liberal System." *Blackwood's Edinburgh Magazine* 16 (1824): 442–455.

Robinson, David. "The Faction." *Blackwood's Edinburgh Magazine* 22, no. 331 (1827): 403–431.

Roosevelt, Franklin D. "Fireside Chat on Primaries." June 24, 1938. *The American Presidency Project*. https://www.presidency.ucsb.edu/documents/fireside-chat-14.

Roosevelt, Franklin D. "Introduction." *Public Papers and Addresses of Franklin D. Roosevelt*. Vol. 7. Edited by Samuel Rosenmen. New York: Macmillan, 1941.

Roper Center for Public Opinion Research, Prevention Magazine, The Tokyo Broadcasting System, et al. "Political Ideology, Three-Way, 'Describe Your Views' (1976–2014)." Roper Center for Public Opinion Research, 2024. https://ropercenter.cornell.edu/ipoll/trend/5040ff44-3006-4322-acd8-01bbe3754efc.

Rosenblatt, Helena. *The Lost History of Liberalism: From Ancient Rome to the Twenty-First Century*. Princeton, NJ: Princeton University Press, 2018.

Rotunda, Ronald. *The Politics of Language: Liberalism as Word and Symbol*. Iowa City, IA: University of Iowa Press, 1986.

Ruggiero, Guido de. *The History of European Liberalism*. Translated by R.G. Collingwood. Oxford: Oxford University Press, 1927.

Russell, George W.E. "A Protest against Whiggery." *Nineteenth Century* 13 (1883): 920–927.

Ryan, Alan. *The Making of Modern Liberalism*. Princeton, NJ: Princeton University Press, 2012.

Samuel, Herbert Louis. *Liberalism. An Attempt to State the Principles and Proposals of Contemporary Liberalism in England*. London: Grant Richards, 1902.

Schapiro, J. Salwyn. *Liberalism: Its Meaning and History*. Princeton, NY: Van Nostrand, 1958.

Schurz, Carl. *Speeches, Correspondence, and Political Papers of Carl Schurz*. Edited by Frederic Bancroft. New York: G.P. Putnam and Sons, 1913.

Schumpeter, Joseph. *History of Economic Analysis*. Edited by Elizabeth Boody Schumpeter. Oxford: Oxford University Press, 1954.

Slap, Andrew L. *The Doom of Reconstruction: The Liberal Republicans in the Civil War Era*. New York: Fordham University Press, 2006.

Slesser, Henry. *A History of the Liberal Party*. New York: Hutchinson & Co., 1944.

Smith, Adam. *An Inquiry into the Nature and Causes of the Wealth of Nations*. Vol. 2. Edited by Edwin Cannan. London: Methuen, 1904. Originally published in 1776.

Smith, Bruce. *Liberty and Liberalism: A Protest against the Growing Tendency toward undue Interference by the State, with Individual Liberty, Private Enterprise and the Rights of Property*. New York: Longmans, Green, 1887.

Smith, George H. *The System of Liberty: Themes in the History of Classical Liberalism*. New York: Cambridge University Press, 2013.

Southgate, Donald. *The Passing of the Whigs, 1832–1886*. London: Macmillan, 1962.

Southey, Robert. "Review of *Memoires de Madame la Marquise de la Roche Jaquelein, ecrits par elle-meme*." *Quarterly Review* 15 (1816): 1–69.

Spencer, Herbert. *Social Statics*. London: John Chapman, 1851.

Spencer, Herbert. "The New Toryism." In *The Man Versus the State*. Indianapolis, IN: Liberty Fund, 1982. Originally published in 1884.

Sproat, John G. *"The Best Men": Liberal Reformers in the Gilded Age*. New York: Oxford University Press, 1968.

Stapleton, Augustus Granville. *George Canning and His Times*. London: John W. Parker & Son, 1859.

Stearns, Harold. *Liberalism in America: Its Origins, Its Temporary Collapse, Its Future*. New York: Boni and Liveright, 1919.

Stephen, James Fitzjames. "Liberalism." *Cornhill Magazine* 5 (1862): 70–83.

Sunstein, Cass R. *Liberalism: In Defense of Freedom*. Cambridge, MA: MIT Press, 2025.

Taft, Robert A. "Liberalism—Real or New Deal?" *Young Republican* 1, May 1936.

Taft, Robert A. "What is a Liberal?" *Commercial and Financial Chronicle* 163, no. 4491 (1946): 2641, 2668, 2670.

Temperly, H. *The Foreign Policy of Canning 1822-1827*. Hamden, CT: Archon Books, 1966.

Thomas, R. Hinton. *Liberalism, Nationalism and the German Intellectuals.* Cambridge: Heffer and Sons, 1951.

Thomas, William. *The Philosophical Radicals: Nine Studies in Theory and Practice, 1817–1841*. New York: Oxford University Press, 1979.

Thomson, Arthur. "'Liberal': Nagra anteckningar till ordets historia." In *Festschrifft tillagnad Theodor Hjelmquist pa sextiarsdagen den 11 April 1926.* Lund, Sweden: Karl Bloms Boktryckeri, 1926.

Trefousse, Hans L. *Carl Schurz: A Biography*. Knoxville, TN: University of Tennessee Press, 1982.

Vallier, Kevin. "Neoliberalism." *Stanford Encyclopedia of Philosophy*. Edited by Edward N. Zalta. https://plato.stanford.edu/entries/neoliberalism/.

Vaïsse, Justin. *Neoconservativism: The Biography of a Movement.* Translated by Arthur Goldhammer. Cambridge, MA: Harvard University Press, 2010.

Vincent, John. *The Formation of the British Liberal Party*. New York: Charles Scribner's Sons, 1966.

Voegelin, Eric. "Liberalism and Its History." Translated by Mary Algozin and Keith Algozin. *Review of Politics* 36, no. 4 (1974): 504–520.

Walpole, Spencer. *The Life of Lord John Russell.* Vol. 1. London: Longmans, Green, 1889.

Warren, Charles. "The Progressiveness of the United States Supreme Court." *Columbia Law Review* 13 (1913): 294–313.

Weiler, Peter. *The New Liberalism: Liberal Social Theory in Great Britain 1889–1914*. New York: Routledge, 1982.

Williams, Raymond. *Keywords: A Vocabulary of Culture and Society*. Revised edition. New York: Oxford University Press, 1983.

Zwolinski, Matt, and John Tomasi. *The Individualists*. Princeton, NJ: Princeton University Press, 2023.

Index

P. de Marneffe, *The Myth of Classical Liberalism*, Palgrave Studies in Classical Liberalism,
https://doi.org/10.1007/978-3-032-14319-8

Kolibri 360 GmbH
Ferdinand-Jühlke-Straße 7
99095 Erfurt, Deutschland
produktsicherheit@kolibri360.de